A
EVERY DAY

How to Rediscover Yourself in Your Story

To Eugenia,

May you be blessed as you venture further into your story!

Blessings,

Elroy Byam

To Meika, Mom, Dad, and Samantha.
And those around the world on a search to find themselves.

TABLE OF CONTENTS

0 | INTRODUCTION

I love looking at model homes – more so, their insides. Growing up, my mother would often get randomly titled magazines with pictures of living and bedroom furniture. I'd look at the furniture and the room and think to myself, "Man, if this room was mine!" The magazines grew into episodes of MTV Cribs, with the celebrities showing off lavish rooms they barely spent time in. I'd look at the luxury homes (except for Redman's – that was horrible), and think to myself, "Man, if this house was mine!"

I was halfway through high school, and colleges were taking their best shots through the mail. I grew up in New York City, so most of these attempts were brochures from CUNY (City of New York) and SUNY (State of New York) schools. At some point I had to select a major. What major allows you to design different homes from the outside in? Architecture, I thought to myself, and so began the journey of flipping through books of suburban homes and residential structures.

Until my third semester of college.

The professor was well into his teaching years and looked like he'd be done with his job by time we started looking for ours. His eyes quickly scanned the class and the ends of his mouth curved upward into something clever – the clever that says 'you have no idea what you're getting yourself into.'

"I hate to tell you guys this, but out of the thirty-something of you in this room, only eight will probably end up as Architects."

It was *Intro to Architecture*, and I laughed on the inside, begging him to take back his blasphemy. He had no idea how hard I studied for this – all the laughter I endured skipping out on lunch with friends for books of luxury home floor plans at Barnes and Noble's. I'm proud to say there were more than eight of my classmates that finished the program. I, however, was not one of them.

By semester three, Architecture wasn't what it was cranked up to be. *MTV Cribs* was dying out by then, and so was my desire to draft floor plans for high-income buyers. I thought I saw the light, but it was just hours of light tables, Exact-o knives, and projects returned with B's and C's on them. My roommate Ben was killing the Architecture game, while I was just killing myself.

One November day, southwest Michigan was unseasonably warm. I kept switching my focus back and forth from my carriage house project to students throwing a frisbee outside my window. They were laughing and talking with each other, and I couldn't make out what they were saying. I would do a "bad lip reading" for one of them, and it sounded like this...

"Elroy, what are you doing here?"

"You're not having any fun in this program!"

"Don't you miss talking to people?"

I had no idea what I was doing there anymore. I was not having any fun. And I did miss talking to people, but what major would let me talk and communicate with people for a living? Communications and Journalism, I thought to myself, and so began the journey of flipping through books of mass persuasion and electronic newsgathering.

One of the first things I learned in my Journalism class was that reporters need to provide the main elements of their stories in five W's: Who, What, Where, When, and Why. Every now and again, How catches FOMO and sneaks its way into the quintet. We're not here to talk about How for now – if you're reading this you've already accomplished that. That being said, here are the five W's for this read.

WHO IS THIS BOOK FOR?

This book is for James. James comes home from work, blinks once and he's in bed, twice and he's back at work again. James doesn't like disappointing his friends, so he says yes to every invitation only to suffer in silence about not having enough time to start his consulting business – the one he's been thinking about for the last two years. This book is also for Christina, who's a senior in high school making A's and B's. Christina grew up in a low-income neighborhood and when she graduates, she'll be the first in her family to do so. Two Ivy-league schools want Christina, but she's not sure whether she wants to go away for college or stay local to look after her mother who's not doing too well. This book is also for Monica, who's in her sophomore year of college and wants to change her major, and Mark, who's 20 years removed from grad school and feels trapped in his corner office on the corner of *Rat* and *Race*. So, for the James', Christinas, Monicas, and Marks, this is for you. And me too.

WHAT IS THIS BOOK ABOUT?

While there are thousands of self-help books out there, I'd like to envision this as a self-*discovery* book. So many of us are trying to make sense of this fast-paced info-based era we live in, but we're just reacting to it all instead of acting towards our goals and aspirations. Those who are winning – the ones we associate with success – are the ones who've taken time to develop clarity on who they are, where they're headed, and where they'd ultimately like to be. Those elements in a nutshell are what make a story a story, but more on that later.

WHERE SHOULD YOU READ THIS BOOK?

Anywhere! At the gym. In the barbershop. On your lunch break. The moment the seatbelt sign comes off on your flight to Los Angeles. And definitely on vacation in Santorini. I don't care - just read it, process the good stuff, and throw away what you don't need.

WHEN SHOULD YOU READ THIS BOOK?

Give this a read when you need a different perspective on the same struggles you're facing. When you look around and it feels like all your friends are passing you by. When you want to be the person in the *after* picture but continue to live in the *before*. When your vision board begins to blur, and the collection of inspirational Instagram quotes wears off. Anytime you need a primer or refresher on where you'd like to be in your narrative, give this a read.

WHY THIS BOOK?

Simon Sinek says that before delivering a product or service, all companies should *start* with WHY, and here I am ending with it. I've read a ton of personal development books over the years (which was and still is great therapy for me) and realize the importance of investing time in yourself. It's not easy to get away from the noise of a fast-paced world, but it's necessary if you want the clarity and energy needed to realign your vision and goals.

After observing an endless array of social media posts, I began noticing a trending message – that in this busy world, we have to constantly post to notify our friends and loved ones that we're still around. I hope this book reminds you of our humanity – that no matter who you are, your story matters in the context of a much larger one.

DO NOT READ THIS BOOK IF

1. **You know absolutely everything.** This is not a book for those who feel they're incapable of learning something new and ingesting new ideas, stories, or concepts. I do not present this as pedagogy, but will posit from personal and observed experiences.

2. **You undisputedly, unequivocally, understand who you are.** If you have a good grasp on who you are, what you've been called to do, and can pinpoint where you are in your narrative, then this may not be the read for you. Feel free to pass it along to someone who's actively searching for themselves or may be unaware that they're unaware of who they are.

3. **You're not ready to make any changes in your life.** This is a fair decision, but only if it's one that you've come to terms with and are comfortable with that determination. This read would do nothing but torment your current comfort and choice to remain the same.

When I switched my major, it appeared that the most successful people in my classes were the ones that always had their hands full. They were championing local causes, leading out in campus organizations and doing everything it takes to impress future employers. My new professors would call their names in class early and often, and they could respond with confidence and assurance. I thought their busyness meant productivity, so I followed suit. Communications Club? Yes sir. Poetry Club? Let's do it. Talent Acquisition for TV projects? Count me in. I finally had my hands full of production projects and extra-curriculars. I thought I had finally found myself, but honestly?

I had never felt more *lost*.

1 | LOST

"When you don't know what's true for you, everyone else has unusual influence." -Stan Slap

There's a meme of Janet Jackson floating around the internet. She looks very distraught - hair frazzled, eyes on the verge of tears. And the caption?

> *Me trying to excel in my career, maintain a social life, drink enough water, exercise, text everybody back, stay sane, survive, and be happy.*

It's amusing. Honest. Relevant. Find the picture online and you'll see that poor Janet looks frazzled and out of order - mainly lost. How do we define lost? I googled it, and the first definition was the best one.

| Unable to find one's way. |

This is the reality for many of us. We act as if we live an accomplished life filled with motivational quotes, travel pics, and smiling families. But under the pretense of our performance lies an infantile cry for help – a need to be rescued from the constant need to matter. At this point, you might be wrinkling your face a bit, telling yourself "I'm not lost, what's wrong with this guy?" If this rings true for you, ask yourself these questions:

1. What was I put on earth to do?

2. How am I adding value to those around me?

If you can already answer these questions, that's awesome – chapeau! For the others, that's ok – my hope is that by the time your eyes meet the end of this book, you'll find yourself, your gifts, and people to share them with.

WHY ARE YOU LOST?

I'm glad you asked. The simplest reason is because as time goes on, you've established yourself as an expert -- in everyone else's narratives. You've spent so much time, energy, and finances in other people's stories and yet somehow have no idea where you are in yours. How do I know this? Think back to when you were around 3-4 years old, intelligible enough to understand *The Three Little Bears*. You're tucked away in your favorite pajamas and blanket and your mother looks at you with her tired, loving, dream-filled eyes.

"Mommy, tell me a story."

Mom obliges, and for the zillionth time, she blesses your ears with *The Three Little Bears*. At 3-4 years old, we already understand that the moments before bed are about processing narratives - we usually don't want it to be our own. Returning to our day requires reflection, and that's too much labor for our child-like mind. So, we skip onto the playgrounds of our subconscious until morning calls. Rinse. Wash. Repeat.

"Tell me a story."

It doesn't change as we get older. We come home from school or work and the same question looms over our heads. We're more mature and too prideful to ask our parents for stories at this point, so who do we ask to tell us stories now? Better yet, what devices do we ask? One is most likely perched on a wall or stand in most living rooms. Another is probably resting in your pocket.

"Tell me a story." On goes the 6 o'clock news, the Lakers game, and a House Hunters marathon.

"Tell me a story." On goes our Facebook, Twitter, and Instagram feeds.

"Tell me a story." On goes Netflix, Hulu, and YouTube.

And while we get our fix, the yawns come, and the deflector shield activates against any attempt to reflect on our day. And this is why we are lost.

If I was a publicly traded company (Chapter 6), it would be my job to get shareholders interested in me by convincing them that I know who I am and where my company is going. But as time goes on, it would also be my responsibility to keep those same shareholders invested in my story. And what better way to keep shareholders invested in my story than by sharing my story every day. It's when we run away from our stories by hiding in other ones that we become lost.

The ability to communicate with anyone at any time through anything has scaled tremendously. The problem with this is that while availability and communication methods have scaled, time has stayed the same. We've prostituted our time to everyone and everything without realizing how much of a commodity our time is.

Remember when email first arrived? People were always checking their inbox to see which of their friends sent them messages. It was cool to spend time reviewing them. Now? Find me a person with zero messages in their inbox! Our world became increasingly noisy. Everybody wants a piece of us and is clamoring for our attention.

What's worse is how people make us feel when we don't tend to their needs right away. I was by my Godmother's house in New York one weekend. She was throwing a small lunch for my sister's birthday. She had recently exited the kitchen and I gave her a tight hug to thank her for the upcoming meal. She gave me a tired smile in return - genuine, but tired.

"Hey Auntie, is everything ok?"

"Yes, I'm fine." She kept her eyes locked on me for a brief moment, then changed her tune.

"You know I send you stuff on WhatsApp all the time and you don't even respond, right?"

Yikes. I could tell she was a little hurt. (Even Godmothers feel it when we don't find the time to reach out and respond!)

"At least you can say hello..."

"You're right Auntie," I responded, and I knew that even though it was coming from just her, I was equally hearing it from everyone else who tries to connect with me there. (Sorry WhatsApp, but after a while, there are only so many 5-min videos and well-wishing gifs one can take in before they have to get back to work.) And if Janet Jackson feels like she can't keep up with everything, then how are we supposed to?

Text messages follow up phone calls. Emails are sent with read receipts. This is modern-day communication gluttony – we haven't tempered our expectations in our relationships and it's draining everyone's batteries. We have the capacity of connecting with millions of individuals, but not enough bandwidth to be intimate with them all. You can't meet everyone's needs at all times because time won't allow it. And it's ok – once you figure out it's ok, you're on the beginning of the journey to find yourself, identify your gift, and share your gift with the world.

THE LATEST FRONTIER

The Challenger Deep is the deepest known point in the Earth's hydrosphere. It's located at the southern part of the Mariana Trench in the Pacific Ocean – not far from Guam. I already have to plug my ears from water pressure when I swim down to 12 feet of water, but can you imagine how water pressure must feel at a dive of *35,000* ft?

On March 26th, 2012, renowned film director James Cameron climbed into his uniquely designed one-man submarine and plunged into the Mariana Trench's Challenger Deep. He was going to explore lifeforms and collect ocean bed samples for science. Cameron was literally immersing himself in another story.

James Cameron said that the Mariana Trench (35,800 ft or seven miles) is the last great frontier of our world. With all due respect Mr. Cameron, I respectfully disagree. Where I do agree with Cameron is his belief that the force that drives all exploration is curiosity, and our curiosity has led us to one of the greatest explorative eras of our time – The Information Age. There's no need to worry about the last great frontier because we're already in it.

I remember creating my first social media profile back in 2005. The moment I was put on to websites like Hi5 and Sconex (last-wave Millennials may have missed out on these!),

I fell in love. You mean to say I can create an online profile of myself and see how many friends I can connect or reconnect with? And we could all be on at the same time and message each other? It was AOL Instant Messenger on steroids, but still manageable. Later that year I would go to college and sign up for Facebook, where back then only 25-30 other people were part of my university's online network. It was still in its infancy and it was cool. People would have actual conversations on each other's profile pages. Back then, no one slid in anyone's DMs. Then Facebook scaled. And networks grew. And people got nosier and more sensitive. Over time, we modified our behaviors to incorporate the newsfeed - an endless waterfall of memes, announcements, political rants, inspirational speeches, and your mother's favorite Bible verse. No wonder we're emotionally unstable - The Frontier has docked on our shores and irreverently planted its flag. In our cubicles. At our dinner tables. In our bedrooms. And we're not quite sure what to do next.

Like space and the deep sea, you can enjoy both from afar. They are museum masterpieces – candy and curiosity for the eyes and mind. Humans don't have the capacity to exist in either place for too long because we weren't designed for those environments. We can venture to worlds unknown, but at some point, we must remember our limit and respect our design. It's the same for social media. So many are vexed with the quality of their relationships. *Fake friends*, they say. *Don't pour into people who aren't pouring into you*, they say. And while there's truth in this, there's an even larger truth. As I mentioned before, social networking has scaled, but time hasn't. It's like taking a large pizza and what used to be an eight-slice experience is now a 32-slice circus. A pizza with eight slices provides quality bites. But how can you enjoy 32 cheese strips? It's the cheese-strip relationships that are killing everyone, and we've all gotten lost in the process.

As we proceed through The Frontier, we need to respect it for what it is - a vast open-world environment meant to be explored in moderation. But how do you create moderation for a Frontier that continues to reinvent itself? There are no rules, no "computer hour" like there was in my childhood. Our escapism addiction has reached an all-time high. The shiny objects are no longer just in the sky, no longer living behind the glass of the jeweler. They are in our pockets, always vibrating and tugging for attention. The sum of our attractions has become distractions.

FEELING ALONE

I'm a first generation African American from Harlem, NY. That being said, the stereotype gods were supposed to bless me with a healthy dose of basketball athletic acumen (handles, a consistent jump shot, etc.) but I think they were off duty the day I was born. This would lead to a series of anxiety-inducing pickup games, breaking the expectations of those I'd never played with before. One bumble of the ball on a fast-break opportunity and I'd practically never see the ball again. If your fellow baller brethren lose their trust in you, you get relegated to the pool of "average" players – the ones you need to round out your team of five when no one else is available. In that world, if you're not great *on* the court, it doesn't create many opportunities for people to know you *off* the court. I would experience this time and time again – the lonely feeling and temperature rising warmly in my cheeks like mutiny against the mind.

People often wandering in their own worlds can be mean. Their lack of emotional intelligence and empathy can push us towards isolation and escapism, traveling deeper into The Frontier of our social feeds. Do you ever get that lonely feeling? The one where everyone and everything around you in the moment seems to know exactly what they're doing and why they're doing it except you? FOMO creeps in, and we quickly want to jump into other narratives not named our own.

It's easy to buy into the lie that you're the only one going through a problem. But that's just what it is – a lie. An illusion. Everyone's going through something. A failed business attempt. A health scare. Low self-esteem. Rebellious children. A fractured relationship. We don't know who to turn to in order to solve our problems, and we feel like we're in this life thing alone. Our loneliness pushes us deeper into The Frontier and as we scroll and swipe, time flies and we never get anything done. And as we feel guilty for not getting anything on our to-do lists done, we dive right back into The Frontier. A vicious cycle.

GUARDING YOUR TIME

Do you ever struggle with finding time to do the things you *really* want to do? It seems like with all of the day's notifications and updates, there's barely any time to gather our thoughts anymore. In a span of 10 minutes, I could receive a call from my sister, 15 WhatsApp notifications, an Instagram tag telling me to watch the video about that guy doing some crazy thing at that place, several 20% off emails, and a reminder that it's my turn to move in *Chess with Friends*. And this could all be just on my commute to work!

When we don't guard our time, we give everyone and everything unlimited access to our well-being. This is the worst thing we can do, because we rob ourselves of agency. We give away our value and enslave ourselves to the beck and call of every notification. This is the usual narrative of the lost person. When you say yes to please everyone with no energy left for self-reflection. I know, because I'm a recovering people-pleaser. I was so afraid of people not liking me and often tied my worth to how loyal I was to their cause. It's hard to guard your time when you don't realize the value of your minutes. Every day, you receive these precious minutes in the form of what I call a *daycheck*, but I'll save that for Chapter 3. When you don't tell those minutes where to go, they'll quickly find another event or task to latch onto.

Not guarding your time on a long-term scale is one way to begin to lose yourself. As you begin to lose yourself, you can also lose the understanding of who you are. How well do you know yourself and the role that you have in life's larger narrative? What are the expectations that you have set for yourself or that someone else has set for you? This book is a call for your freedom. I'm hoping you answer this call. Some people don't have the freedom they desire because they're not willing to spend time in the areas where they need the most development. So how do we free up more of our time and discover the narrative we'd like to live?

For those of you who don't know what cache files are, they are temporary data files stored from apps that make it easier to navigate through the app the next time you open it. These are helpful in the short term, but over time slow down your computer's performance by taking up too much space. Clearing cache files helps free up space on your computer and can speed up performance. Like computers, sometimes we can have too many tabs open in our life at one time. We feel like we're missing out on events, so we make ourselves available for everything. How are our brains supposed to perform at optimal levels when we don't take time to clear the cache files of everyone's expectations of us?

THE SEARCH FOR FREEDOM

Ever since I was a kid, I loved reading. One of my favorite children's books was called *Finding the Green Stone* by Alice Walker. The story is about a young boy named Johnny who lived in a town where everyone owned a shiny green stone. Johnny's not on his best behavior, and as he acts out one day, he loses his green stone, sending his entire family and town on a frantic search party. As he searches for the stone, the metanarrative begins to clear – he is also searching for himself.

We are all searching for something. We can spend the lion's share of our day in cubicles, knee-deep in numbers and non-sense, chained in between paydays like a corporate version of Prometheus. Our minds search for other worlds and narratives – ones that love us for who we are and appreciate the value of our time and attention. If you don't know by now, *attention* has and always will be your greatest currency. That's why when your parents or instructors ask you to "pay attention," they sub-consciously drive the notion of focused time having monetary value.

We need to be more aware of the narratives we direct our attention towards. Our search for freedom demands a level of awareness that something in your story needs to shift. For those of you who drive stick shift, you're well aware of your commutes as a series of shifting gears. There are seasons where first gear is adequate and others where sixth gear is a must. But you can damage your clutch or stall out if you stay in the same gear for too long. Sometimes we need to envision a new narrative in order to wriggle out from under the weight of an old one.

HOW DO WE FIX THIS?

Some time ago, a fight broke out between two young men in the streets of Atlantic City. A group of friends surround-ed them -- laughing, instigating, and egging them on. Ibn Ali Miller was 26 at the time, and driving by, noticed the scuffle. Within a couple minutes he calmed the storm of rambunctious testosterone, informing them that he knew a few of their parents – some currently locked away, and not to bring shame to them.

"I'm not leaving here until I see y'all shake hands. Shake hands."

The unit of youngsters laughed at Ibn as he relentlessly worked to disarm the duel. Some time went by, and after a few more attempts to provide peace, guess what? They shook hands.

Ibn is rare. When conflicts appear out of nowhere, we are either afraid or entertained. We'll grab our phones and document the experience but won't do much to alleviate it. This results in continued brokenness for those in conflict – their struggle encouraging us to laugh or leave. But Ibn did something special that day. He saw the conflict and was neither entertained nor afraid. He saw kids that reminded him of his own. Kids that were lost and trying to find their manhood through folly and fisticuffs. He saw something that was broken and took time to fix it. Many times, those "somethings" are somebodies and those somebodies are us.

If for one moment we can admit that we're lost and broken in a world of noise and narratives, we may have a chance to fix ourselves. So how exactly *do* we fix ourselves?

- We have to understand that we are (or were at some point) *lost* (Chapter 1)

- We have to understand *story* and where we are in our own narrative (Chapter 2)

- We have to be grateful for the value of our time and guard it relentlessly (Chapter 3)

- We have to be aware of the cycles in our story and how to use them to our advantage (Chapter 4)

- We have to get away from everything we consider familiar to develop and nurture a new perspective (Chapter 5)

- We have to retool our new perspective into a life-changing mission (Chapter 6)

- We take on this life-changing mission and serve the world (Chapter 7)

"Tell me a story."

No matter how you spin it, everyone loves a good story. This is the ongoing appetite of our brain. When we wake up and catch the news. When we're at work by the water cooler. When we're in transit on the way home. When we unwind with our friends, spouse, kids, and loved ones. When we're moments from closing our eyes for as long as our subconscious will let us. What we're really asking for is to:

"Tell me how someone like me got through their situation so their struggle can give me the strength to get through mine."

It's time to find ourselves again, but before we do, we first have to understand how stories are told.

2 | HOW TO TELL A STORY

"There is no greater agony than bearing an untold story inside of you."
-Maya Angelou

I was born in the late 80s, late July, and late at night. My mother taught nursery classes at a private school in Manhattan's Gramercy Park district. Every day, we would take two trains to this school where we would learn and experience things quite disparate from my zip code.

One day the school closed down and I was sent to my "zoned school." Some zoned schools have high GPAs and spirited PTA meetings. My zone school laughed at me for not knowing who Master P was and punched me in the face only two days in. This began a series of "high voltage" culture shocks - powered by hip-hop, Timberlands, and brown-skinned girls with PCJ perms. Wrestling moves, wedgie excursions, and fisticuffs. I would die over and over again, only to be revived with a little more convergence. My "hellos" became "wassups", my high-fives became daps, and my orange off-brand boots? Well that took another couple of years.

Finally, by 8th grade I had become pretty fluent in Ebonics. I knew just enough to stay out of trouble and just enough "Yo Mamma" jokes to not get punked. I ran the newly discovered lingo through high school like a charm and have been "bilingual" ever since.

What I just explained to you about myself is an example of what's called The Story Spine.

THE STORY SPINE

Out of all the extracurriculars I got involved in during college, one of the best ones I joined was an improv group. I remember learning various improv games – being excited about the idea of resetting the story and character over and over. It was all fresh, exciting, and freeing. I even used some of what I learned to make up bedtime stories over the phone with my now-wife, Meika!

What I'm about to share with you is not new. It has been told many times over in our lives. You're living it right now and don't even know it. A playwright named Kenn Adams created it in 1991. I first heard about it in the fall of 2008, when I tried out for that improv group in college. Our instructor Bryan told us that we were going to make up a bunch of stories using a special narrative sequence called the Story Spine. The Story Spine is the chronological layout of events that follow this sequence:

Once upon a time, there was...

And every day...

One day...

Because of that, because of that, because of that...

Until finally...

And ever since that day...

Most stories we know follow this sequence. Let's apply this narrative sequence to a story you've never heard of until now:

Once upon a time, there was a town where animals lived in harmony with humans. Each one loved and respected the other. And every day, each animal used their natural talents to help the humans. The otters would finish their meal and swim in fast circles around the lakes, which generated and stored power for the entire town. The birds would fly overhead and sing in different notes throughout the day. Some notes were in the tune of 'good morning' to those heading to work, others were 'cheer up' to those feeling down. Sometimes, the birds sensed the change in weather and would sing notes of incoming rain or snow, letting the humans know to be careful when they were outside. Each animal had its own way of helping the humans get through the day, season, and year. Each animal, except for Tiny the Elephant.

While all the animals had their own kind to live, work, and play with, Tiny the Elephant was alone. And not only was Tiny alone, he was extremely big and clumsy.

"Look, there goes Tiny!" an otter would say, and spit bursts of water towards him as he walked by a lake. Tiny would sigh, and as he kept walking, his steps were so heavy that it would send tremors into the water, messing up an otter swim cycle and a power outage took place for a few moments. Tiny would sigh. The adults would sigh. Their kids would sigh.

"TIIINNNNYYYY!!!" The president screamed from the top of the highest building.

"Welp, here comes Tiny!" a bird would say, as the flock was flying overhead, singing about rain. They would try to get the rain message to the humans, but Tiny was so huge that the message in the sound waves changed as it hit his body. Rain would come, and that part of the town was none the wiser – soaked and shivering as they left their offices thinking the birds had sung 'nice and sunny.' Tiny would sigh. The adults would sigh. Their kids would sigh.

"TIIINNNNYYYY!!!" The president screamed from the top of the highest building.

Sometimes the sighs were so loud that Tiny would leave the town for the countryside – sitting in an open field and stuffing his face with dandelions.

One day, a group of otters swam in circles in a lake much faster than usual. The power plant was overflowing with electricity, which supercharged an underground powerline that was connected to the highest building. A fire broke out in the highest building, and the humans inside started to scream. The otters from that lake and others tried spitting bursts of water towards the highest building, but the water only went as far as they had spit it towards Tiny. The birds tried all the songs they knew, but they had never sung about fire before – there had never been a fire in the town until that day.

As the fire continued to make its way up the highest building, humans quickly make their way down and out. All humans that is, except the president, who worked at the top. Humans called for the fire department from the next town over (there was no fire department in town), and by the time they came, the fire was more than halfway up the building. All around on the ground of the highest building, humans and animals sighed. The adults sighed. Their kids sighed. One of the birds peered into the top of the highest building and saw the president, scared for their life.

"Faster!" The birds sang to the humans in the fire department, as their ladder extended from the truck. But when the ladder fully extended, it was two floors short of the top of the highest building. None of the other humans and animals knew what to do.

Far out into the countryside, Tiny was full from stuffing his face with dandelions. He was just about to take a nap, when his big ears heard a group of sighs coming from town. Tiny couldn't feel any worse about himself, as the sighs were the reason he would go to the countryside. He looked in the direction of town in sadness, but as he looked, he saw huge billows of smoke in the center of town. It looked like it was coming from the highest building. Tiny was surprised, and immediately got up on all fours and stampeded his way towards town.

When he got to the edge of town, he passed by lakes where the otters played. He passed by patches of sky where the birds sang. He had never gone towards the center of town where the highest building stood. Humans and animals watched as he sped on by, windows from nearby buildings shattering from his steps. By the time he got to the center of town, most of the humans and animals were there, watching the fire fighters hose down the flames. Tiny looked at the highest building and could hear the president at the top.

"TIIINNNNYYYY!!!" The president screamed from the top of the highest building. He could see the large elephant all the way at the bottom, far larger than all the other animals and humans.

Tiny thought for a moment, then took his trunk and began to stretch it towards the top. It stretched up past the ladder where the firefighters were. Up the extra floors where at this point all the birds were flying around the top in a circle and singing. It wasn't a song about for the morning, or feeling better, or the rain. It was a song for Tiny.

"Tiny... Tiny... Ti-NY! TI-NY!"

At the bottom of the highest building, the rest of the animals and humans chimed in.

"Tiny... Tiny... Ti-NY! TI-NY!"

Tiny's trunk continued to stretch upwards until finally it broke through one of the windows at the top of the highest building, grabbed the president, and pulled the president to safety at the bottom.

Everyone cheered in applause for Tiny the Elephant. The adults cheered. Their kids cheered.

"TIIINNNNYYYY!!!" The president screamed from the bottom of the highest building. The president cheered and gave Tiny a special medal with a message that he was always welcome in town – no matter how big or clumsy he was. No other human or animal had received a medal that special before. The fire died out with much damage done to the building, but everyone that was once in the building was saved. And ever since that day, Tiny the Elephant was loved by all humans and animals in town.

What a day for Tiny the Elephant, huh? That's his tale, but now let's look at the Story Spine in the context of your story.

ONCE UPON A TIME

This is the start of your story. The main setting where you and the supporting characters are introduced to the audience. On a macro level, this could be the day you were born. On a lesser-scale level, it's the first day of high school, or the beginning of that ad agency job on Madison Ave.

But just because you started in one place doesn't mean you have to stay there. You could not control where or how you were born. But you can control a lot of what you do in the time that follows.

AND EVERY DAY

This book was titled *And Every Day* for a reason. These are the habits and routines that you and your supporting cast members undertake to establish character distinction. Everything you do in this part of the story sets you up for the *One Day*.

I can't stress enough how important this part of the Story Spine is. There has to be a structure developed if one day you have plans to open a business, author a book, or get married. Your *One Day* will never come if you don't put enough emphasis on your *And Every Day*. Better yet, *One Day* could come, and you won't be prepared for it because of the deficiency in your everyday activities.

I hated Kobe Bryant. I never watched him in his afro years, but it didn't matter because I hated Kobe Bryant. That championship year in the 01-02 NBA season when he and Shaq ran through Jason Kidd, Keith Van Horn, and the rest of the New Jersey Nets? From that moment on, I hated Kobe Bryant. I wasn't even a Nets fan, but they were so close in proximity to my New York Knicks that it felt like the Knicks would've won if they won. But they didn't. And for the next 15 years, I hated Kobe Bryant.

That is, until his final game.

On April 14th, 2016, the late Kobe Bryant found the fountain of youth for the last time and ended his career with a 60-point gem. It was a majestic, other-worldly performance by the Black Mamba. He had willed his team to a come-from-behind win, beating the Utah Jazz 101-96 at a star-studded Staples Center. Shaquille O'Neal, Derek Fisher, Robert Horry, and many Laker greats were there to tip their hats and pat the back of the man who poured 20 years of excellence into the game of basketball. The time hit triple zero. The crowd went ballistic. And yet I still hated Kobe Bryant. Then the reporters came over and asked him if he was going to relax in his first day of retirement. And here's how Kobe responded:

"That's a slippery slope. I've done some research from players post-career, and it goes, 'Tomorrow, tomorrow, tomorrow.' Then all of a sudden it's 'Uh-oh.' The important thing is to get into a routine, to maintain discipline..."

He continued:

"I've been in a routine my entire career. The worst thing I can possibly do is not have one because then you wake up without a sense of purpose, a sense of direction. I have to find a routine, get into it and be comfortable with it."

The worst thing I can possibly do is not have [a routine]...

And it was after he said these words that in some weird, light-bulb-on kind of way that I became a Kobe Bryant fan.

You cannot fall in love with being mediocre. Adobe's 99u conference is an annual event for creatives to not just create ideas, but make their ideas happen. At their 2014 event, speaker and author Todd Henry said, "Mediocrity doesn't just happen. It's chosen over time. Through small choices, day by day." It's the day-to-day, often mundane choices that if left unattended march us towards being average. If we are not driven by purpose daily, then we are competing for complacency.

On any given week, you can find folks on Facebook who share how draining their workweeks are and how they can't wait until Friday. I will agree with them in principle but not in purpose. The end of the week usually indicates rest – a cessation from the campaigns within the cubicle. But I do believe that how we feel on Wednesday morning is just as important as our mood on Friday afternoon.

Some people's routines are setting them up for failure. They come home, and Netflix tells them what to do before bedtime. Little by little, they develop a reputation.

Steven Furtick, lead Pastor of Elevation Church in North Carolina's Charlotte region said: "Your reputation is the result of your routines."

FINANCIAL - And every day, Martin would put away $1 from his allowance in his piggy bank.

PHYSICAL - And every day, Caroline would go to the gym at 5am.

SOCIAL - And every day, Keisha DM'd people on Instagram for collaborations.

MENTAL - And every day, Will would spend five minutes speaking affirmations to himself.

Be cognizant of how you're spending your time and energy in your everyday routines. What do your routines say about you to other people? To yourself? How do your routines and habits set the stage for the next part of your story? Because no matter what, there will *always* be an interruption in your story, for better or worse. And what you do every day will be an indicator of how you respond to it.

ONE DAY

This is where the narrative gets more serious and where the rubber meets the road. Where an opportunity arises, or catastrophe ensues. How you respond to this phase greatly depends on whatever you did in your *And Every Day* phase.

FINANCIAL - One day, Jim saw a new game system for sale at the local toy store...

PHYSICAL - One day, Veronica took a look in the mirror and found herself 15 pounds heavier...

SOCIAL - One day, Karen received a DM from the digital strategist for Will Smith...

MENTAL - One day, Sean accidentally stepped on his bully's new shoes during gym class...

Every page of your story, for better or worse, matters, so stop ripping up pages in your story. They're there for you to learn so you don't make the same mess in the next chapter.

BECAUSE OF THAT, BECAUSE OF THAT, BECAUSE OF THAT...

After two years of marriage (once upon a time), a husband and wife are trying to get pregnant. They've been doing their "due diligence" for the last 6 months (and every day!), but to no avail. One day, the wife is teaching 10th grade math when she tells her students she'll be right back. She heads to the bathroom and barely makes it through the first stall where her bowels erupt out of her mouth. She slowly tries to gather herself, and as she makes her way up from the floor, she erupts again.

"Are you alright, Ms. Sanchez?"

A few minutes must have passed, since Tiffany entered the bathroom and noticed the wife on her knees in her bright purple flats under the stall.

"Yeah, I'll be fine."

Later that evening, the wife is back in the bathroom – her own this time – wiping away tears of joy as she sees a second stripe appear on her recently-purchased pregnancy test...

Because of that is where the conflict *really* begins. This is where the interruption in your story unravels through a series of fortunate or unfortunate events. Kenn Adams, creator of the Story Spine, says the *because of thats* are the middle of the Story Spine's structure. The everyday routine is broken, and several events follow. These events make us wonder how things will end up for the character(s) we've invested interest in.

I believe that there will always be good and bad conflicts in our story. Good conflict is the up and down of dumbbell curls during weight training. It's the tied game at the bottom of the ninth, two outs, full count. Good conflict says, *I can't wait to see how this all unfolds, and I have to go through this current experience to find out.* In the first installment of *Rocky*, Rocky Balboa *had* to go pound for pound with Apollo Creed to complete that part of his story spine and begin another narrative, also known as *Rocky II*. Many of us are afraid of good conflicts, because they require us to stretch in areas we'd rather leave dormant. It's easy for us to push good conflicts to the side and become lured into conflicts that have nothing to do with us – the narratives that don't need our focus and attention. Me writing this book is pushing through good conflict because I know I have to massage this message over and over again until it's ready for you, the reader.

Let's return to our husband and wife story. We'll change the characters to a guy and girl who are dating and in their second year of college. They've been together on and off for two years – both have commitment issues and even find it hard to commit to their academic programs. Throughout their second semester, the guy and girl find themselves in a lot of "extracurricular activity" – the kind that doesn't show up on resumes. But what *does* show up one April day the week before finals? The second stripe on a pregnancy test.

The wife crying tears of joy is now replaced by the girl crying tears of frustration. She's immediately frustrated with the guy for not being more responsible and then becomes frustrated with herself. What did she do? Why didn't she say no all those other times and stick to it? How is she going to take care of a little one when she could barely take care of the egg from *Economics 101?* This is what I call bad conflict.

Bad conflict is messy. Bad conflict is the character assassination of employees in your workplace. It's the brackets around the numbers in your bank account. It's the meaning in what's often unsaid versus what is. Many people have created cultures around bad conflict because that's all they've ever known. Drama is their oxygen, and if they don't experience bad conflict for some time, they'll do whatever it takes to create it.

In the summer of 2012, my wife Meika and I were still dating. She was living with her parents and working at their practice in Southfield, Michigan. One afternoon, she came back home to a flooded basement – a few inches of water filled every nook and cranny. She immediately called her father and he told her that the sump pump was probably broken.

A sump pump is a small pump placed in the lowest part of a basement. It's designed to keep lower areas of homes and buildings dry and prevent them from flooding. When water flows into the sump pit (via drains or water migration), the sump pump pumps the water out and away from the home or building so the lower levels stay dry.

Think of your mind as a sump pump. When bad conflicts arrive and try to flood your attention, you can filter the conflict and redirect it out and away from your nerves. If you don't take care of the sump pump, the conflicts will come and flood your foundation – your ability to make clear decisions and control your emotions.

Because of that is the bridge that begins at the interruptions in our story. On that bridge, we build character, and learn how to deal with conflict. The good news is that the story spine doesn't allow us to remain in this part of the sequence forever. The sun always has to set, and eventually rise again.

UNTIL FINALLY

Have you ever been on a long drive and constantly asked, "Are we there yet?" I guess no one really says that anymore because our smartphones have GPS apps with ETAs. How about when you're waiting for a package to arrive in the mail, and you keep checking to see if you get an email update or text? *Until Finally* is the climax of the story. It's the moment in *Lord of the Rings: The Two Towers* where Gandalf finally arrives at the battle of Helm's Deep (*first light on the fifth day... at dawn, look to the East*). It's "Luke, I am your father!"

Every story has a climax – the highest point in the journey where there are ooohs, ahhs, and gasps. We ask ourselves, is the character ok? Did they defeat their antagonist? Did they overcome the obstacle and get to their destination? Was there victory or defeat? It's why many of us binge watch entire seasons of shows in a day – we want to know how the characters' stories play out. *Until finally* validates the prior settings, routines, interruptions, and unraveling events that follow. No matter how tough or easy your current road is, the season in your story MUST come to an end.

EVER SINCE THAT DAY

Across my slowly aging frame are several scars. One strike on my left hip is from a 5th grade pickup game, where I ended up sliding across the asphalt trying to get a loose ball. Another one rests on the top of my left hand near my index finger – I was taking the last waffle out of the oven and getting ready for 7th grade homeroom when all of a sudden, the top of my hand hit the inside ceiling of the oven. All on the last friggin' waffle!

Further up my left index finger lies a scar from a cut I never thought would heal. I was wrapping up a study tour in college and was traveling on the Euro rail from Venice to Florence. Bread and butter arrived at our car, and it wasn't long before I began cutting across one of the rolls until I wasn't cutting the roll anymore. I had sliced right into my index finger and was met with a very red response. I quickly got it bandaged and feared that I'd need stitches or would never see my finger the same way again. *Ever since that day*, a scar appeared in the form of a small frown, a sad footnote on an otherwise wonderful academic adventure.

Ever Since that Day doesn't always have to bear scars of horrific events. It could be the "after" picture of the body you want to have, place you'd like to travel, and home you want to live in. It's the fulfillment of dreams after lots of goal-setting and hard work. In this part of the story spine, the old events have passed on and have made way for new ones to take place. The cycle is now complete, and *Once Upon a Time* is ready to take shape again.

THE CHARACTERS IN YOUR NARRATIVE

One of the first video games I ever played was *Super Mario World* for Nintendo. For the seven or eight of you who don't know who Mario is, he's a fictional character trying to save Princess Peach from Bowser, the evil Koopa king. Bowser repeatedly kidnaps Princess Peach throughout the Mario franchise and Mario continues to save her to restore peace to the Mushroom Kingdom. Along the way, Mario receives help from several characters or powerups that allow him to advance through the story. Like Mario, there are characters in your narrative that you must be aware of at all times in order for you to progress through your story. These characters fall under *protagonist, antagonist*, and *supporting cast*.

A protagonist is the main character of a story. They are usually at the center of the story and their decisions affect how the story plays out over time. In many cases, they are the hero – called to action by a larger purpose, wrestling with that purpose, navigating through adventure, confronting their nemesis, and declaring victory or defeat as a result. In most stories, the hero comes out victorious and will return home – forever changed by their prior experience.

YOU are the hero of your story. You have a golden opportunity to go on an adventure, identify and sharpen your skillset, vanquish your villain, and change the world. None of this adventure comes without risk. Adventure calls you out of your comfort zone, and because most people like comfort, their actions and behaviors keep them in their situation. You should not be so focused on preservation that you forget about progress.

What good would any story be if the hero didn't have a nemesis? Who would Luke Skywalker be if not for Darth Vader? Or Simba without Scar? What merit would good have in this world if it wasn't working to overcome evil? Nothing good comes without its challenges and obstacles. And that's where the antagonist comes in.

The antagonist is the rival of the protagonist. They arrive in the hero's story for one reason – to take out their mission. In some of our stories, the antagonist is easy to identify and out in the open. The 2nd grade bully. The Debbie-downer. The neighborhood gossiper. They are all in place to impede your progress physically, financially, emotionally, mentally, spiritually, and any other "ally" that requires growth.

There are also times when the antagonist is well-hidden in presence or mission. Absent from your sight, this kind of antagonist will watch your journey from a vantage point and wait for the best opportunity to strike. Like the Wicked Witch of the West, they'll document your yellow-brick progress from the sidelines, plotting for the best moment to take you out. They cannot stand what you stand for and will celebrate every stumble in your journey towards your goals, hoping you will surrender.

The hardest antagonist to identify is one with a hidden agenda. They may be in your inner circle – family members, friends, and loved ones. They may even be unaware they are antagonists – impeding your progress in the name of their comfort, leisure, and entertainment. I personally believe many people are on edge today about their relationships because they find it hard to detect who is on their side and in their corner. Those close to your heart may be aligned with you in presence but not always in purpose. They love being near you but not the vision given to you. This can lead people down a dark spiral of fear, mistrust, and discontent – keeping everyone at arm's length. If executed well, this belief eventually pulls the antagonist's best trick out of their hat. The belief that everyone (including yourself) is your antagonist. And that the conflict in your story remains forever, without a resolution.

If you are reading this, remember: YOU are the protagonist and hero of your story. Like Super Mario having powerups and creatures to assist him through each level, you also have a supporting cast. These are people who will sacrifice their space, time, money, and attention for the success of your mission. Do your best to identify your supporting cast and add value to them throughout your endeavors.

Be careful of abusing your supporting cast as they venture alongside you to defeat your villain. During our climb towards success, we can view our relationships as transactional – yes-men and women to our beckon calls for support and other resources. Once we no longer view them as valuable, we forget about them and the fact that they are also protagonists in their own narrative. It is extremely important to be aware of your inner hero and how you are called to a greater destination than the place you're comfortable in now. Also, be aware that you are a member of someone else's supporting cast – that as much as you need human benevolence, there are those that desire it from you. And finally, be aware of your inner villainy, the dark side of yourself that could be impeding your progress or the advancement of someone else.

WHAT MAKES A GREAT STORYTELLER?

I knew one grandparent, vaguely. My mother's mother spent most of her life in the Caribbean, venturing to the United States ever so often in her later years where a few of her children emigrated. She passed when I was 16, and my inner journalist mourned not being able to extract more stories from her when I had the chance. I was more focused on my Game Boy Advance than my grandmother the last time I saw her – and once she went, so did a million laughs and tears.

Those that were (and still are) fortunate to spend time with their grandparents know that they don't just arrive to your home with gifts, goodies and ginger candies. They also come with stories – the ones that make your belly ache from laughter, arrest your attention, and send you off into your dreams. These are the stories that stay with you, generational heirlooms that you can pass on to your progeny. I'm going to go out on a limb and say that grandparents are great storytellers. But what is the anatomy of a great storyteller?

A great storyteller understands why. On February 7, 2018, Nancy Pelosi set a record for the longest continuous House floor speech. She spoke for 8 hours and 7 minutes on stories of DACA recipients in an attempt to protect laws and federal funding for them. She spoke from 10 am eastern time to shortly after 6 pm eastern time, standing in four-inch heels and never took a break for water or relief. According to House floor rules, leaders are allowed to speak for as long as they please, and Nancy took advantage.

Like Nancy, great storytellers connect with *why* they're telling the story and because their passion shows, they draw believers further into their tales. Great storytellers aren't just confident about their connection to the story, but also its chronology. They know the ins and outs of every sequence and can describe them with gestures and gusto from beginning to end. We all know at least one individual waiting with bated breath to insert "you know, that reminds me of a time when..." in every conversation. This is a gift, but not always utilized well during interpersonal communication. Know how you'd like your story to end and get there.

A great storyteller begins with the end in mind. Peter Nowalk, creator and executive producer of the ABC hit show *How to Get Away with Murder* illustrates this concept by premiering each of the show's seasons with a murder scene. Every episode builds on the timeline leading up to the catastrophe, and the viewers eliminate potential suspects in a whodunnit style. When you're telling stories, build them in such a way that your viewers and listeners are always asking "what happens next?" Assume this notion for both your audience and yourself. After admitting to yourself that you're lost, think about how you'd like your story to end. Whether it is today's conflict, the current season you're in, or your life in general, ask yourself that same question – what happens next?

If a man courts a woman, he may begin with the end in mind. He may think of how the woman would be as a prospective life partner, picturing scenarios of going through the years with them in various situations. They envision what the end could look like and based on that end they craft their approach. Who or what are you trying to court? What reality are you envisioning for yourself? Sometimes it's hard to envision a reality outside of the one we're in because we've been bricked in by our own conflicts.

I challenge you to lean against those bricks as hard as you can with positive affirmations. You *are* strong. You *are* worth it. You *are* valuable. You *are* enough. Lean into those bricks until they crumble, and you can use them for the road ahead. Paint the bricks yellow. Then take the first step.

WE ARE ALL GRIOTS

I am no expert on griots and griot culture and am glad to introduce you if you're hearing about this term for the first time. *Griots* are historians and storytellers originating from the West African countries. They are responsible for carrying the history, genealogy, and cultural traditions of their village from one generation to the next. Music is also involved in their storytelling, as various instruments and notes are played during their recitations. Without griots, stories and genealogies of generations die. Villages lose access to their history. Villagers lose access to themselves.

We are all griots, so to speak. Our stories have meaning and it's our job to preserve them and pass them on. Who would our parents and grandparents and great-grandparents be if they didn't arrest our attention with their stories? As we age, we begin to accumulate many stories. Stories of birthdays, bullies, and late summer nights. Stories of sleepaway camps, Christmas dinners, and broken hearts. Stories that take up memory in our memories. Stories we wish we could remember. Stories we're still hoping to forget. We have the agency to choose the stories we want to bring to the surface and believe about ourselves. The ones that give us hope and remind us that our birth was not an accident. That we do have purpose. I'm hoping you discover or rediscover that purpose, but in order to do that, you have to learn how to guard your stories.

And also, your time.

3 | THE DAYCHECK

"The quality of your life is directly affected by how and where you spend your time." -Lee Cockerell

I remember when I received my first paycheck from my first boss, Mr. Phipps. He is a tall man with a warm heart and at the time was responsible for the maintenance operations at my local church in Harlem. After a few weekends of scrubbing toilets, vacuuming sanctuaries, and mopping fellowship halls, he stood in front of me and four other colleagues with some envelopes. He scanned the envelopes for names and began distributing them to their rightful owners. When he got to mine, he looked into my eyes and with a sage-like grin, said, "Here you go, young man." One hundred and twenty dollars of legal tender lived in that envelope, and my 14-year-old mind couldn't wait to spend it on DVDs and Pepe Jeans. And unfortunately, that's exactly what I did.

A paycheck is the currency you receive for your work – usually calculated by an hourly wage, salary, or gig. I'm sure there are many people who count the days to their next payday or even the day they can start working towards a paycheck. It's nice to feel warm and fuzzy on payday, but who wouldn't want to get a paycheck in their hands or bank accounts *every* day? What if I told you that we already are? Well, sort of. Those who are hourly employees for organizations are paid in correlation to the number of hours worked while salaried employees have yearly salaries divided into a series of weekly, bi-weekly, or monthly payouts. This is what we call money – dividing people into several socioeconomic classes and castes. Money is one asset of life, but we often forget about *time*.

Money comes and goes, but we can never replace time. Once a moment passes, it can never be relived again – only reimagined or reminisced. Time is the great equalizer. While people have varied salaries and statuses, every day, *everyone* gets 24 hours. These 1440 minutes are what I like to call a *daycheck*. The reason why I call these minutes a daycheck is because it allows me to wake up and be immediately grateful for a gift I don't deserve. I didn't work for it. But if I wake up and realize that my day, being, and presence have meaning, I can view every day as a gift. Many people tend to view their Friday afternoons as a gift, but not Monday mornings.

A PRETTY NORMAN LIFE

Let's pick a random guy from humanity and call him Norman. If you know Norman, I promise you it was just a coincidence. Norman works 40+ hours a week for a tech startup doing UI/UX design work. His boss is a visionary but very demanding of his time with tight deadlines and deliverables. Norman has a wife and 2-year-old daughter who both wish they could see more of him when he's home, but he's so drained upon arrival. His wife is frustrated because she wants him to spend more time with his daughter, and when Norman gets home, he divvies up his time between winding down, playing with his daughter, and maintaining intimacy in his marriage. Oh yeah, and let's throw in a tri-color Beagle named Eagle, just for kicks!

Here's a look at Norman's Daycheck:

6:00a | Wake up

6:00a – 6:15a | Walk Eagle

6:15a – 6:30a | Check on daughter

6:30a – 7:00a | Shower + get dressed

7:00a – 7:30a | Breakfast for three

7:30a – 8:00a | Morning news + family time

8:00a – 9:00a | Leave for work

9:00a – 5:00p | Work

5:00p – 6:00p | Leave for home

6:00p – 6:15p | Greet wife/Walk Eagle

6:15p – 6:30p | Check on daughter

6:30p – 7:30p | Wind down

7:30p – 8:00p | Dinner for three

8:00p – 8:30p | Clean-up/Chores

8:30p – 9:00p | Put daughter to bed

9:00p – 10:00p | Time alone/Intimacy

10:00p – 10:30p | Shower and get ready for bed

10:30p – 6:00a | Sleep

This is how Norman's daycheck is divided on an average workday, with a few hours give or take to put his daughter back to bed at night when she has trouble sleeping, or when he's summoned to draft an app concept for a client over the weekend. Norman wants to audit his daycheck to see where he could get more time alone. Right now, the equation of Norman's alone time looks like this:

2 hrs of transition time + 1 hr of wind down time = 3 hrs alone time

Norman has 1/8 of his daycheck to himself. If you discount the transition hours of his driving to and from work, then he really has just one hour. One hour! I'm sure there are many people and parents like Norman who feel like they don't have much time to themselves. Babies spit up. Pictures fall down. Family/friends call. Disasters strike. And somehow, we become the only Ringling Brother in the circus who has to juggle it all. Poor Norman – he probably feels like our Janet Jackson meme from Chapter 1. If I could, I would ask Norman to do an audit. Could he do seven hours of sleep instead of eight? If so, he can get back another hour of his daycheck by starting his morning at 5a before Eagle the Beagle wakes up, or ending his day at 11pm, after his wife's love cup is full. With a quick audit, we've given Norman one extra hour to his day by taking away one hour of sleep.

Our daychecks may not look like Norman's. We may get the same minutes, but they're distributed differently. Sometimes we say we have no time for anything, but that's because we're afraid of evaluating where we spend our time and what we're doing with it. Like money, if you don't tell your time where to go, boredom, people and other variables will control it for you.

One of my favorite quotes is from a man named Stan Slap. He's a New York Times bestseller and specializes in manager, employee and customer cultures. When it comes to having a clear vision and proper time management, Slap says, "When you're not on your own agenda, you're prey to the agenda of others." *Yikes*. This hit me square in the face when I read it, because it zeroed in on my struggles with saying "no."

For a long time, I was a "yes" man. I cringed at the idea of someone not liking me for turning them down, saying no to something, or just being blunt. I believe this led to a series of people, places, and positions that took up valuable portions of my daycheck, and once they were satisfied and their "thank yous" were distributed, I was often left drained, empty, and further away from where I wanted to be with my goals. Then again, could I clearly identify my goals or agenda? If not, it would be easy for me to become wrapped up in someone else's.

As your daychecks add up, they should be in the direction of a clear agenda and vision orchestrated by you. If not, you'll be going in circles – enslaved to both your past battles and present behavior. It's alright to serve and do things for people, but you must know *why* you're serving and whether it's in alignment with your principles or long-term goals. If not, you might want to start learning the art of saying "no", but we'll talk about that in a little bit.

Looking for more time in your day? Evaluate your daychecks down to the minute:

1 Daycheck = 24 hrs = 1440 minutes.

Every day we get paid 1440 minutes, and the real question is, what are you doing with yours? Once you get a good grasp of your 1440, you'll be much more aware of the market that's clamoring for it.

MY DAYCHECK: THE SEVEN WS

I haven't mastered my 1440 yet, but I've broken down my ideal daycheck into a series of what I call the Seven W's: wake up, worship, workout, write, work, wind down, wonderment. Remember, this is my ideal within a proposed workweek structure, and the minutes from my daycheck will vary for each W depending on what's needed for the day.

W1 | WAKEUP | 5:00a – 5:10a. Here begins the day. I rid myself of eye crust, morning breath, and yesterday's urine as best as I can within ten minutes.

W2 | WORSHIP | 5:10a – 5:30a. Once I've given myself the first ten minutes of my daycheck, I give the next 20 to a higher power. For me, that is God. For others, it could be meditation or just sitting in silence.

W3 | WORKOUT | 5:30a – 7:00a. After feeding myself spiritually, I can work on myself physically. The workout portion really lasts for 1 hour, then I shower by 6:30 and get dressed around 6:45.

W4 | WRITE | 7:00a – 7:15a. By 7a, I should be dressed and ready to go. Within these 15 minutes I can choose to write, watch some news, or make a quick smoothie.

W5 | WORK | 7:15a – 6:45p. Let's say my work commute is 45 minutes. Since this is free transition time, I'll catch up on a podcast or call a family member. I get to work for 8a, and "crunch the numbers" until 6p. Same activity driving home, where I should arrive by 6:45p.

W6 | WIND DOWN | 6:45p – 11:00p. Here's where the free-for-all begins. Once I'm home, I have to decide what's most important for the next few hours. Dinner? The Knicks game? My wife? Eating dinner while watching the Knicks game *with* my wife? *Wind down* varies for different folks depending on the season they're in. I had to spend a lot of my wind down time writing this book! If my ideal daycheck checks out, I should be in the shower by 10p and then by 10:15p I'm in bed with a good book or random puzzle app with way too many ads between games.

W7 | WONDERMENT | 11:00p – 5a. This is the tax I pay out of my daycheck to my rejuvenation, tax that gives me energy to receive the next check. After pouring myself into the world outdoors and pouring into my family at home, it's time to recharge. Some people's batteries recharge in 8 hours. For me? Six to seven is fine. For now.

I'm very grateful for my daycheck and if you're reading this, you should be grateful too. Somewhere, someone is counting on you to identify your gift and add value to them. Every day, your account gets restocked. 1440 minutes. And what you do with those minutes can change the trajectory of your life and story.

❖

THE MENTAL MALL

On August 11th, 1992, The Mall of America opened up in Bloomington, Minnesota. It boasts 520 stores and attracts more than 40 million people every year. Imagine the amount of time it would take to visit each store long enough to make a purchase! Malls are places where people hang out when they're either bored, dating, or need some retail therapy. At least that's what used to happen, but for all intents and purposes let's believe it is still so.

Every day, someone or something wants a piece of your daycheck – more so your attention. You instantly wake up walking into what I'll call the *Mental Mall*. This mall is replete with businesses designed to grab your attention with brand awareness, sales, and beautifully fashioned storefront windows. As you get out of bed and proceed through your day, here are some of the most popular stores in the Mental Mall:

THE KIDS STORE

This store is filled with breakfasts, boo-boos, and bear hugs. Babyproofing, baseball games, and bed-time stories. The Kids Store doesn't close. It's a constant adrenaline rush and designed for parents to always be aware of what their child wants and needs at any moment of the day. Sometimes parents spend so much of their daycheck in the Kid Store that they don't have many minutes left for the Spouse Store, or the Self-Discovery store. (By the way, this book is found in the Self-Discovery Store, so thanks for stopping by!)

THE FAMILY STORE

Similar to the Kids Store, the Family Store comes with aisles of parents, siblings, and relatives that need a favor, advice, or your listening ear. The Family Store will sometimes tell you how to run the Kids Store or will often wonder why your Mental Mall hasn't opened a Kid's Store yet! Their flash sales come in text messages, group/video chats, phone calls, and any form of reminders to stop by the Family Store and see what's new if you haven't been there in a while. If you don't budget minutes in your daycheck for the Family Store, be careful – they may guilt their way in!

The amount of time spent in the Family Store will depend on your principles and mission. It will vary from culture to culture. Some people don't have a Family Store in their Mental Mall because they can't go in and walk out without chaos. The Family Store will often remind you of where you came from more than where you're headed, and sometimes space is needed. Plan your trips accordingly.

THE FRIEND STORE

Not too far from the Family Store lies the Friend Store. Some Mental Malls even have mergers of the two franchises, and you'll find a few "Framily Stores" as a concept. The Friend Store is filled with good times, mutual support, and affection. You must provide personal support as you move around the store – often making sure you show up for the major and minor events. But the investment in those store minutes provide great returns around birthdays, weddings, funerals, and other events where crowdfunded support is needed in time, finance, and attention.

People are sometimes confused by The Friend Store's marketing tactics because their storefront windows change more often than desired. But if you understand that the Friend Store has ad hoc committee meetings to assess relationships with their customers, you'll understand their reasoning. There will be friends who love you for what you say 'yes' to, and who will question their relationship with you by what you say 'no' to. They won't always understand or agree with your agenda, but if they're really in your corner, you'll know by how they respond to your successes and failures over time. They won't mind your absences too much if you add the right amount of value and support when they need it. Real friends understand that you have a daycheck just as much as they do and will respect your wishes to skip a visit to the store every now and again. Just don't walk past the Friends Store too many times without a check-in or one day you may find a "Closed for Business" sign.

THE SOCIAL MEDIA STORE

This store is designed for connection and engagement. It's the Grand Central Station of all other stores in the Mental Mall, connecting them in an endless network of noise and notifications. This store often competes with the Kids Store depending on how old the kids are. Boasting flagship products like

Facebook, Instagram, YouTube and Twitter, The Social Media Store is the new foundation for FOMO (fear of missing out) – constantly selling you on the idea that something is going on in areas you're not, and that you need to be there. Without monitoring, heavy amounts of your daycheck are spent in this store and at the end of the day, you're wondering where all your minutes went.

Sometimes we spend our daychecks at The Social Media Store because we haven't told our minutes where they should go and what they should do. When we understand how to monitor our minutes to advance our stories for good, then we can make wiser decisions with our time.

Everyone's Mental Mall is set up differently and while we have the same daycheck, our minutes won't be evenly distributed. Now that you're aware of these stores, I want you to become more aware of how you're spending your daycheck at them. Your attention is an asset, and it's needed more than ever if you're going to get on the other side of your dreams and goals. Changing how you utilize your daycheck will require a major culture shift, and in order to make that shift you have to figure out your current culture.

WHAT'S YOUR CULTURE?

I LOVE the holiday season. When November begins, I start to think about shorter days and longer nights. Mac and cheese and sweet potato pie. Family colloquy. Snowflakes, lighthearted Target ads and Pentatonix albums. These sensory experiences have become part of my 4th quarter traditions and thoughts – my culture, as it were.

The late philosopher U.G. Krishnamurti once said, "Society or culture or whatever you might want to call it, has created us all solely and wholly for the purpose of maintaining its continuity and status quo." I do believe that society comes from "maintaining its continuity and status quo," and is often its own enemy. To me, culture is the repetition of actions and behaviors that are eventually accepted as normal. This acceptance happens at various levels. We accept these behaviors ourselves when we expect them and don't receive much resistance at the conscious level. When our body and mind are in sync for a gym workout, or we eat specific holiday foods, we are either creating or continuing culture. We accept these behaviors in our ethnic cultures whether we play music at loud or low levels, throw commemorative birthday parties at 15 years old, or have a high tolerance for spicy or salty foods. And we accept these behaviors in larger geographical cultures when our country has a national language or how astonished some people may become when they see others that don't look like them in their country.

Try and take some time to observe some of the cultures around you:

WORK CULTURE

- How effective is communication at your workplace?

- Is your boss or supervisor aware of what motivates you?

- Do your colleagues assume responsibility for their actions?

HOME CULTURE

- Is your home usually clean and presentable? Are things put away in the right place?

- Does your home have music always playing in the background?

- Does your home have a particular scent from plug-ins, candles, or incense?

RELIGIOUS CULTURE

- Do you attend a house of worship every weekend?

- Are the same people sitting in the same seats at your house of worship every week?

- Do you meditate with a group of people on a specific weekday?

FAMILY CULTURE

- Is there a family member everyone goes to when there's conflict?

- Does your family all live within 25 miles of each other?

- How often to you communicate with your family members throughout the day, week, month, and year?

For me, I've challenged my ethnic and societal cultures for most of my life. I was born in Harlem, New York, but did my early schooling in Gramercy as my Mom taught at a private school in downtown Manhattan – different school district, different culture. I love the city, but I also love the country and outdoors. (I still get laughed at to this day when I tell my friends I'm going hiking or kayaking!) The more I've leaned into the cultures I thought I was supposed to fit into, the more I felt like I wasn't being myself. I realized that I have cultural and experiential roots that are in Harlem and many neighborhoods beyond. And quite frankly, there's nothing wrong with that.

As you make observations about what's orbiting around your sun, I ask you, what's your culture? What are the actions, habits, and behaviors repeating in your environment that you have accepted as normal? Take a few notes on your current state of mind and what's become normal for you. What have you adopted as truth that could be changed? Your culture can be changed; it's completely up to you. But first, you have to fix your core.

WHAT'S AT YOUR CORE?

Growing up, I remember doing sit-ups and realizing that every time I would do sit-ups, curling upwards would produce a small "air mountain" right above my belly button. All through my college years I ignored it and thought it was just stomach fat that needed slimming. One day, I decided to check it out. I Googled something about why my stomach was sticking out while doing sit-ups, and like every other situation we're concerned about, others had wondered about their stomachs as well. Turns out I had what was called *diastasis recti*.

Diastasis Recti is the thinning of the linea alba which connects the two sides of your abdomen. This thinning leads to a gap in the area where the abs meet up and form that nice six-pack, causing some individuals' stomachs to poke out or look pregnant. Many mothers experience diastasis recti post-partum and have to do various exercises to restore their core. *Restore their core.* Sign me up, because from the looks of it, my core was never together.

For many of us, at the center of our daycheck lies our culture, and at the center of our culture is our core. Every good and strong culture has a great core. We see it in sports all the time. The New York Yankees dynasty in the 90s had Derek Jeter, Andy Pettite, Jorge Posada, and Mario Rivera, known as the "Core Four." They didn't earn that title on day one, but over years of clutch hitting, pitching, catching, and closing out games. In the NFL, Tom Brady and Bill Belichick have been at the core of the New England Patriots' domination of the AFC since 2002, and it hurts for me to say that as a New Yorker! In the NBA, we've seen core dynasties like Kobe and Shaq on the Lakers in the early 2000s, Tony Parker, Manu Ginobili, and Tim Duncan on the Spurs in the mid-2000s, the new "Big Three" Celtics of Paul Pierce, Kevin Garnett, and Ray Allen in the mid to late 2000s, Miami Heat's Big Three in Lebron James, Dwyane Wade, and Chris Bosh in the early 2010s and in the mid to late 2010s, Steph Curry, Klay Thompson, Kevin Durant, and Draymond Green of the Golden State Warriors. All of those teams were championship teams that developed strong cores.

Most of our body's movements are connected to the strength of our core. We need a strong physical core in order for us to stabilize ourselves in a turbulent environment. Not just physical, but mental as well. People will say mean things about you. They'll act as if you don't exist. You'll be placed in situations where every facet of your character will be tested, baiting you for your most incendiary response. Only if you have a strong core will you overcome the walls, obstacles, and villainy.

Having a strong core also means having strong principles. And strong principles come from strong decision-making. You must know when to say "yes" and "no" and not worry about the outcomes.

Ray Dalio is CEO of Bridgewater Associates, one of the largest investment companies in the world. He is also one of Forbes top 100 Wealthiest People in the World and one of Time Magazine's 100 Most Influential People. In his book *Principles*, Dalio says that the way we see things and the people we're connected to affect where we go in life. We'll also constantly be in situations where we'll have to choose if we're going to put others' interests above our own or vice versa. Without a strong core and solid principles, our daycheck will always be up for grabs from the wants and needs of other people. Dalio further states that people have a hard time achieving success because of their emotional responses to some of these situations. He writes on how most people move on emotions within the moment, and that they go from one emotional experience to the next. That, to me, does not sound like "strong core" behavior.

In layman's terms, having a strong core is really connected to your perspective on life and how you emotionally respond to what life sends you, which can be defined by your principles. Start listing off your principles. What do you stand for? What *can't* you stand? Can you control your emotional response to whatever makes its way into your story? If you want something in the current chapter of your story to change, you have to *believe* that it can be changed.

PROJECT X = WHY

In August 2015, I kissed the Cinderella Castle. I quickly planted my lips on the side of the cold edifice like I was tucking it into bed for the night. (Weird, I know, but I had to do something memorable)! My wife and I were celebrating our 2nd wedding anniversary and were getting ready to leave Walt Disney World's Magic Kingdom in Orlando, Florida. It was my very first time - my mother wouldn't prioritize theme park passes for herself and two children, so I had to wait until I "came of age." And that age was 27. Walt Disney was such an inspiration for me, and his vision and ability to create amusement for both young and young-at-heart still moves me to this day. I mean seriously, who doesn't believe that *The Lion King* is the best animated feature of all time?

I personally believe that with all of Walt's animated and creative achievements, his greatest feat was his ability to take one of the world's most feared creatures and use it to become one of the most beloved. A statue of Walt holding the right hand of Mickey Mouse graces the front of Cinderella's Castle at Magic Kingdom – a tip of the cap to "the most magical place on earth." But this most magical place would've never taken place without some foresight and clever planning.

It was the late 1950s and Walt Disney faced a big problem. He had not bought enough Anaheim land surrounding his beloved Disneyland. Not long after the theme park opened in California, non-Disney-owned businesses capitalized on his success. They opened up restaurants, hotels, and other small tourist attractions that poked a hole in Disney's vision for a fully contained family-friendly community for people to maintain, work, and live in.

At the turn of 1960, Walt began a top-secret mission looking for a second location to take his vision to another level. After seeing the large swamplands of central Florida along Interstate 4, he began what would be a series of mass land purchases under various dummy corporations – over 27,000 acres of land. Who would think that businesses like Tomahawk Properties, M.T. Lott and the Latin-American Development and Management Corp would all be connected to Walt Disney? Emily Bavar, a reporter from the *Orlando Sentinel* figured out that Disney was behind the purchases after several employees provided evasive responses upon questioning. In October of 1965, the *Sentinel* ran a story with the headline, "*We Say: Mystery Industry is Disney*". Hayden Burns, then governor of Florida, confirmed Disney as the mystery industry shortly after the newspaper ran the article. This led to an official public announcement by Walt, his brother Roy, and the governor a couple months later, further confirming plans to build an east-coast version of Disneyland.

On October 27, 1966, Disney recorded a 25-minute video about his beloved Florida Project, formerly known as Project X. This video laid out plans far bigger than Magic Kingdom, Animal Kingdom, Hollywood Studios, and EPCOT. As a matter of fact, EPCOT was the main focus of his east-coast vision, acronymized as the Experimental Prototype Community of Tomorrow. Throughout the film, Disney casts a vision for a city that would trump any other American city in terms of urban planning and development. "Everything in this room will change time and time again as we move ahead. But the basic philosophy of what we're planning for Disney World is going to remain very much as it is right now." *Basic philosophy*. Principles. A core. A culture. An innovative use for someone's daycheck as a future resident of this "community of tomorrow". Walt Disney would never see his plans come to fruition, as lung cancer would take his life in December 1966. Five years later, on October 1st, 1971, Magic Kingdom would open as the first theme park of Walt Disney World, with Roy adding Walt's name as a testament to his vision.

I had never known the difference between Disneyland and Disney World until I got older. I would have never been able to smooch that structure without the mind of someone seeing it there long before I did. The creative cartoonist from Kansas City cast a vision and culture for the land before he decided to change the world. Before you define the world, define the *land*. What is your Project X? And what is the culture that you've subscribed to that's blocking access to you completing your project?

At some point, we have to stop telling ourselves stories that aren't true. The ones where we're too fat, too skinny, too pale, too dark, or too poor. We have to escape stories that make us believe we'll never be free of old scars and new nightmares. We'll have to stop judging the struggles of others and celebrate the possibilities that they (and you) can change. Hopefully soon, more of us will be courageous enough to enter rooms of creativity. Ones that are far away from familial bullies and keyboard warriors. Ones that will draw dream-filled conclusions to chapters not yet lived.

WHEN DAYCHECKS BOUNCE

I have never written a check in my life – well at least at the time of me writing this. To be honest, I've had only one checkbook, but I was too young and broke at the time to have any use for it. I'm not even sure where it is and quite frankly, I don't care. Not with websites and apps where you can send money immediately. Even though there are different ways to send money, our daychecks have remained the same. Every day, another 1440 minutes enters and exits your time bank. Every day, another opportunity arises to advance your story.

Since I've never written a check to anyone, I haven't experienced the pain of someone telling me (or not telling me) that the check bounced. That the funds I thought were there was wishful thinking and not enough. Our daychecks bounce when there are too many events on our plate. When we tell our daughters that we'll make it to their track meet, but our boss stops us in our tracks. When our friends text us about their milestone birthday parties and our family members host fundraisers on the same night. These are all mishaps in our Mental Malls and something's got to give, because we only have so many minutes and moments to live those minutes in.

Our world is suffering from UADD – Undivided Attention Deficit Disorder. Like checks, we may not have the time to give to our loved ones right away, and we make promises as empty as our bank accounts. It's almost like we have to borrow attention on credit. Chasing after your dreams and goals will require intense attention. People will be upset, because you've either broken your promises or their expectations, but sometimes this is what's needed to move out of your current struggle and into a new normal. And the less you make promises you can't keep, the less your daychecks will bounce.

A NEW NORMAL

I remember a conversation I had with a friend some years ago. She was frustrated over an incident with her significant other. They weren't seeing eye-to-eye on a few matters and she felt like her perspectives weren't being considered. This wouldn't be the first time we were having this conversation, and recalling a conversation further back, there were similar tones of unhappiness and concern about their relationship at a macro level. This time it was just a different individual. I looked in her eyes and saw traces of confusion. It was as if she was in shock that she found herself in a similar place with a different face. I decided to prod a bit.

"Can I ask you a question?"

"Sure." I knew she wouldn't be ready for what I would ask next.

"How would you feel if you were in a relationship with someone who more often than not made you feel like you were accepted, heard, and loved?"

"Hmm..." She stopped for a moment and disappeared into her thoughts.

"I honestly don't think I know what that would feel like..."

Accepted. Heard. Loved. These should all be human rights, something that spreads and goes on easy like peanut butter. The problem is, so many of us have grown up in environments facing the opposite. Ostracization, lack of self-worth, and fear became our normal, as our parents and legal guardians could only keep the villain's voice out of our ears for so long. When we duel our first villain, they scare and scar us. They convince us that we're unwanted, unloved, and will bring fear to the rest of the world. And we spend the rest of our lives wandering, wondering, and hoping that everyone we meet isn't as afraid of us as we think they are.

Like my friend, our normal becomes chock-full of broken dreams and unmet expectations. Of paycheck pains and daycheck drains. We sign up for a lifetime subscription to our problems and when the issues arrive, it's bittersweet. Bitter because of how it makes us feel, but sweet because it's a taste our minds have acquired. This is why for those that aren't financially stable or literate, they will quickly spend any excess cash on anything just to bring them back to the story they're used to living in. If you feel like you never have time to do anything, the moment you get a burst of free time, you'll most likely find a way to spend it until you get back to what you consider normal – not having any time.

I believe that there can be another reality for you. One where every matter doesn't involve your emotional response or daycheck minutes. I believe you have to come to terms with the possibility that your story can change. You have to believe that your subscription to chaos can be canceled. And you don't have to invite your old villains into new chapters.

We are all looking for meaning. We want to connect with people through shared experiences and feel safe to be ourselves in the process. When we don't feel safe, our fear causes us to shrink from the decibel level of our villain's voice. We don't believe that we are powerful beings and that our presence has merit in this world. Meaning comes when we finally decide to believe in a better normal. It's that prompting that reminds us that there are people out there waiting for our courage to serve them. But we won't know how to serve them if we remain lost.

If we don't know where we are in our story. And if we disregard the sacredness of our own time.

As I learn more about my own narrative and purpose, I smile because I'm more aware of my life being a journey with the agency to make decisions for better or worse. Every day gives me a new opportunity to change the micronarratives in my current chapter. I've identified my core, which is love and creativity at high levels. When I'm in environments that don't replicate that, I can choose to respond with frustration and fear, or decide that what's to come can and will be better than what is right now. Train your mind to believe that your story will be better than what it is right now. It all starts with a large dose of self-awareness.

4 | THE KNOWLEDGE CYCLE

"Most people waste the best years of their life waiting for an adventure to come to them instead of going out and finding one. They succumb to the status quo and dream of life being different someday. Plagued with indecision, they wait, unsure of the right path to follow. And as they wait, they miss an opportunity to live." -Jeff Goins

In March of 2019, nearly 10 years after being drafted into the league, MLB phenom Mike Trout landed the (at the time) largest deal for any professional athlete in American sports history. He penned a contract extension with the Anaheim Angels for 12 years and - wait for it... $426.5 million! Imagine what 400 million+ dollars could do for a person, a family, a community! But in the world of the modern-day athlete, with their uncanny ability to perform at an extremely high level and fill stadium seats and stands, this was well deserved. Two-time AL MVP. Seven-time All Star. Generational talent. And he's put that talent to good use many times – one time being so unique that only 323 other players had pulled it off in Major League Baseball's 150-year history.

On May 22, 2013, then 21-year-old Michael Nelson Trout became the first player of the season to hit for the cycle and the youngest to do so since MLB Hall of Famer Mel Ott in 1929. For those of you don't know what "hitting for the cycle" means, it's when a baseball player hits a single, double, triple, and homerun all in the same game. This is no easy feat. The player who hits for the cycle spends some time on first, second, and third base, and has to figure out how to advance themselves to the next base while the next batter is up. Hitting a homerun allows them to advance and dance around the bases in one smooth number - the batter's head held high, the pitcher bested by their brawn.

Your ability to achieve what you desire most in life is based on your ability to hit for the cycle again and again. The way I see it, those that operate in places we deem successful – the places beyond the gatekeepers, beyond our fears – have hit for the cycle as many times as they can imagine. Anyone can do the same, but they have to understand how to hit for the cycle in their own game.

Play ball! Imagine your entire life is a baseball game. You're on the field and need to score as many runs as possible for a better quality of life. This life can be whatever you desire - better health, more money, more time with family, more service towards humanity, deeper relationships, the list goes on. Life is the pitcher; the challenge is the ball. The bases are waiting for you to round them, but first you have to believe that you can actually reach the bases. I'm going to break each base down for you, so leave the dugout and step up to home plate, because your name has been called.

FIRST BASE: AWARENESS

Think about a situation you're in, the reality of whatever is happening with you or your current environment. What do you know? What do you want to know? What would you like to change about your situation? Awareness is always the key. The ability to be self-aware is powerful. It puts you in control of your emotions or at least in the right direction of doing so. Self-awareness provides insight into the being that is you. It helps ground you and prepare you for how to respond in various situations. Knowing who you are is a weapon that always needs sharpening, one that you can use for protection against insecure thoughts, feelings, and actions. No human being can or should be more aware of who you are than you. Once you're aware, congratulations! You've hit a single. Welcome to first base, where you've put yourself and your team in scoring position. But you can't stay on first base forever.

SECOND BASE: ACQUISITION

Once you're aware of what you'd like to see change about a situation, you need information and wisdom to properly sort it. What information do you need to assist you with this change? Where can you go to get this information? Who do you need to speak to or surround yourself with? What environment do you need to immerse yourself in to absorb this information? Knowledge is ubiquitous in this age of information. You can now search for information on anything, which can almost always be found in a book at your local library, bookstore, Google, or YouTube. If you have access to the Internet or are in walking distance from a place that houses books, you have no excuse of reaching second base. The answer to any question can almost always be found in between the pages of a book or online. Once you've absorbed as much info as you think you'll need, you have to advance to third base.

THIRD BASE: APPLICATION

This is a harder base to reach than first and second but probably the most important. What's the point of having knowledge if it's never applied? Moving from second to third allows you to move from pundit to practitioner. How do you put what you've learned in motion? Your situation is soon to change in one direction or another, because you've taken what you've learned and put it into practice. This can happen consciously through testing or subconsciously through cultural habits - picked up over time from your environment, accepted as normal by you and/or your community, and applied over and over again for better or worse. Third base puts you in a real position to score, but no one ever scores until they reach home plate.

HOME PLATE: AUDIT

Home plate is the most important advance of them all. You can be aware of something, learn how to make a change, and apply what you've learned, but you'll never get anywhere without reviewing how it went. The audit is the journey home, the scored run, the internalization of how the process went, and if it's worth doing again. As you audit, you must ask yourself more questions. What did you learn? What changed? How have you become a different person as a result of applying what you've learned? The more questions you ask, the more you become aware of what works and what doesn't. The more you become aware, period. And that newfound awareness gives you permission to advance to first base again, all the wiser, all the more changed.

There are reasons why so many of us don't hit for the cycle. Those reasons are rooted at every base, doing everything in their power to prevent you from advancing. I'll call them, *Fear Forces*.

The Fear Force at First Base causes you to sit around and complain about everything - from finances to health, politics to toxic relationships. It works hard at making you believe that nothing can be changed about your situation unless someone else steps up to the plate. Friends have to stop being fake. The President must do better. The rich keep getting richer while the poor...you know the rest. Everyone else is responsible and at fault for why the situation is the way it is. Except you. And the longer you believe you're unable to contribute to the change, the more you'll complain. The Fear Force has done its job with you at home plate striking out again.

The Fear Force at Second knows you're aware of the situation and does everything in its power to make you believe you can't do anything about it. It feeds you the lie that you're helpless, incapable, and insufficient. It convinces you that someone else has all the answers and should solve the problem, but not you. It provides comfort in laziness and supports your unwillingness to learn and gather valuable information. *They're* the smart ones, not me. *They're* the ones that have the know-how, let *them* fix it, not me. The Fear Force at Second is good at leaving people stuck on first. These are the folks that are always aware that something needs to be changed but stay frustrated because they won't take time to learn how to change their situation. A friend of mine said that while she worked at Disney, employees were told when someone asked them a question and they didn't know the answer, "Don't say 'I don't know.' Instead, say 'let me find out.'"

The Fear Force at Third is a popular one. It's the one that laughs at those who are chock full of head knowledge but too scared to practice what they preach. The folks at second can spend a lifetime acquiring information, but what good is it if it's never put into play? Many know this Fear Force to be "analysis by paralysis." It persuades you to keep your head in all the books, podcasts, video content and just stay there. Never experimenting, never testing, never getting your work into the world. And you remain convinced that it's easier to just acquire the knowledge rather than apply it.

The Fear Force at Home Plate plays a dual role. For those stuck on third, it plays to the insecurity of individuals, communities, and organizations that are audit averse. People and organizations will know they need to change, gather the information needed, put that information into play, but then won't take the time to analyze if what they executed on was successful or not. The other role is the most powerful of all roles from previous Fear Forces. It works tirelessly to convince people to remain in the dugout, cheering or jeering all other players while they never step up to the plate for an at bat. When we give up hope, when we lose belief in what could change, when we punt all possibilities of progress and purpose, we painstakingly tell the world that we don't matter.

Congratulations, you're now aware of the bases you need to reach to advance your narrative, along with the Fear Forces that hinder your progress. Now let's see how we can apply the Knowledge Cycle to several circumstances.

EDUCATION

We never really finish school. As the years go by, the desks, teachers, and classmates change, but we will always be in the middle of a lesson. And it's our job as to whether we will apply what we've learned. For those who are in school and want to set themselves up for the next chapter of their story, let's get you on base.

First Base: You're aware that better schools are out there. Ones that look good on report cards and resumes. Schools that place you on short lists for the next greater learning experience. You believe you can attend one of these schools and know that it requires excellent grades and high standardized test scores. Your grades aren't excellent, but great enough that you can make them excellent before the end of the school year.

Fear Force at First: *But those schools are too hard to get into! The education system is already working against you. There's no point in thinking about those schools since you'll probably never get into any of them anyway. Only geniuses and legacy students get into those schools!*

Second Base: You begin drafting a list of the top three schools in your area. If you're in high school, this list has the top 3-5 schools in the country based on your field of interest. You set a dedicated time every day after school for homework, studying, and taking practice standardized exams.

Fear Force at Second: *But not every smart and studious stalwart of a student gets admitted! You'll be missing out on hanging with friends and other social experiences, and for what? For the small probability of admission? It will take too much time and too many books for a chance of too low an admission rate.*

Third Base: As the school year nears the end, your GPA increases. You join the debate team. You take the standardized test and pass with flying colors. That creates the impetus for you to apply to the top schools and take a standardized exam. And guess what? You score in the 90th percentile, and a couple of the top schools accept you!

Fear Force at Third: *The test is too expensive. You're extremely smart but not smart enough. Where are you going to get the money to go to this new school? Forget the test and application. It's not worth it.*

Home Plate: As you're preparing for the first day of your new school, you look back on the entire process. How did it go? What did you learn about yourself, along with the education system? Was it all worth it? And what are you aware of now about school that you can pass on to yourself, friends, loved ones, or your community?

Fear Force at Home: *This was too tiring of an experience to try to pass it on to anyone else. Who would want to hear about your journey anyway? It's crazy that you even got in while still maintaining some of the friendships you had. Why would you want someone to go through the challenge you did? Let's just put all of this behind you, ok?*

RELATIONSHIPS

Relationships are an ever-evolving phenomenon. Rules get written, rewritten, and then thrown out as a whole. People connect, gain trust, fall in love, throw things at each other, share experiences, and cry over gallons of spilled milk. Letter writing was once normal, and now? Texting and DMs. We are all in great need of connection. And this need of connection comes in many stages of relationships. For my single folks who are interested in rounding the bases (as far as the knowledge cycle is concerned!), it's your time to bat.

SINGLE (AND READY TO MINGLE)

First Base: You've been a lone ranger for some time now. You're beginning to entertain the idea that you'd like to be in a mutually exclusive relationship with someone else. You're equally aware that you overthink things like this because your parents' marriage or lack thereof didn't work out well. You feel the anxiety rise whenever someone's interested in you but want to overcome it with new experiences.

Fear Force at First: *Why would you even try dating? You don't look as good as you think you do. You can barely keep your weight down. Who's actually going to be interested in a dull, anx-*

ious, overthinking person like you? There's a reason why you're still single. Live with it.

Second Base: You start researching about meet ups, social mixers, and speed-dating events. You talk with a therapist about how you currently feel about dating along with two close friends and triangulate their thoughts. You listen to several podcasts about the sexes and how their minds work when it comes to dating.

Fear Force at Second: *You can't be serious. That outfit looks hideous! Do you really think when the bell rings that someone's going to want your number? Do you believe you're going to arrest those folk's attention at that meetup? Quit while you're ahead, there's a great Game of Thrones marathon on...*

Third Base: You sign up for a credible dating site and get matched up with three people in your first week. Over the next two weeks, you meet with these people at local eateries. You tell yourself to breathe, relax, and practice other things learned from that relationship podcast you found a few weeks ago.

Fear Force at Third: *They're not going to want a second date with you. You made a complete fool of yourself and laughed way too much! Why did you even go on those dates anyway? No one finds you worthy enough of a long-term relationship, remember? And to top it all off, two of the three dates looked like they were ready to leave...*

Home Plate: It's true. The first two matches weren't feeling the vibe halfway through the date, but the third date wants to see you again. They thought your laughter was refreshing after coming out of a long-distance relationship that didn't bring them joy anymore. The heat slowly began rising in their heart after you traded good-byes that evening. And just like that, your third date wants a second date.

Fear Force at Home: Why would the first two dates not be interested in you? Was it something you said or did? You must've laughed way too much, and they won't even realize that it was because you were nervous. It's only a matter of time before you fumble the fantasy of the one who's interested in you. Because of that, you shouldn't even respond to them when they message you on the site...

MARRIAGE

First Base: You've been married to your spouse for five years now and it feels like forever – the only thing is that forever can't arrive fast enough. The fire that once burned in earlier years has now been reduced to embers. You're aware that something is off and has been off for a long time. You're also aware of your best friend recently getting a divorce, and how you don't want that to be your situation. You sit your spouse down one day when they get home from work, share how you feel about the marriage, and ask if they'd like to go to see a counselor with you.

Fear Force at First: Your marriage has been over for a long time; can't you see that? They don't look at you the same way they used to. They barely mention your name to anyone outside of the house unless asked, and you do the same. It's over, just find a good divorce lawyer and let's get this process started. You don't even have kids together which will make the break so much cleaner.

Second Base: You find a marriage therapist – it was a recommendation from another friend who's been married one year longer than you. You begin going with your spouse to therapy once a week for eight weeks. Throughout the sessions, you learn that your spouse is having a hard time connecting with you – that over the years you're not as fun, outgoing, or romantic as you used to be. The therapist hears both you and your spouse's side, then gives you both homework.

Fear Force at Second: *Who goes to marriage therapy anymore? You already know how hard it is to get your spouse to pay attention. What's going to make this any different? While your spouse is not a dog, you "can't teach an old dog new tricks." You're wasting time, and this is just another fight in the making.*

Third Base: You begin the homework recommended by the counselor. You increase your romantic gestures towards your spouse with longer hugs and more intentional kisses. Once a month, you implement a "$20 Date Night," where you go to the local supermarket and buy things not usually on your grocery list up to $20. This particular date night has you both coming home with fish sticks, plantain chips, Twizzlers, cheeseballs, hot pockets, and pistachio ice cream. And nothing but laughter ensues as you put it all together...

Fear Force at Third: *This is stupid. Homework is for students and you're not in school anymore. And "$20 Date Nights" are for people in school. Why are you buying all this junk? How on Earth do you believe a pack of Twizzlers will save your marriage?*

Home Plate: A week after the final counseling session, you and your spouse get together and have an impromptu "bonus session." You begin sharing all of the things you've learned over the last eight weeks. You realize your spouse is smiling more, and as much as you might not want to admit it, you are too. You find out that your spouse doesn't really need all of the wild fanfare from the romcoms, but really enjoys just spending quality time with you. You realize that work and personal leisure were taking precedence over your marriage, so you stopped answering emails after a certain time in the evening and blocked off time in your calendar to just connect with your spouse. It looks like your spouse's love cup is full. You both end the impromptu session. And begin "another one."

Fear Force at Home: *Aren't you glad that the sessions are over? You barely learned anything you hadn't known before. Now you can never say you haven't gone to counseling and you'll never need to go again! These sessions were mainly for them anyway, not you. They're the ones that wanted to go, not you. Now we just have another person that knows our personal business.*

And speaking of business...

BUSINESS

It's the beginning of June. James has recently completed his sophomore year of college. He's almost home. Sights of the quad, student center, and bookstore are now replaced with basketball courts, barber shops, and corner stores. He turns his key into a 7th floor apartment door. It was a few hundred miles away from his dorm but never far from his heart.

"Jay-Jay!"

Before he pulls his second piece of luggage into the apartment, James' two younger siblings barrel into his waist, offering the only gifts they could afford to muster up at their age – a hug. James returns the love, then looks past his brother and sister to see a woman twice his age sitting on the living room sofa a few yards away. She was peeling some potatoes and watching *Jeopardy*.

"It's about time. I've been waiting for you for two hours."

The woman finally breaks her rhythmic gaze from Alex Trebek to the potatoes and is now fully focused on James. There's fatigue in her eyes, two shifts' worth, but love and concern nestled there too – all fighting for the lion's share of her dwindling attention.

"I know Mom, I'm sorry – my train got delayed."

"It's ok – come let me get a good look at you."

James makes his way past his siblings towards his mother, leaving his luggage by the door. *Jeopardy* goes to break while they embrace.

"You're starting to fill out. Must be all that cafeteria food."

"That and the gym. I do work out now, you know."

James' siblings run towards their rooms in a cacophony of giggles. He could now pick up the smell of fried rice coming from the kitchen. It was the beginning of summer and James needed a job. His mother also needed James to find a job, as his father passed away almost two years ago – right before he left for college...

First Base: A few days later, James starts wondering what he could do over the summer for some extra cash. He has around $200 left over as a refund from his college account. He sets a goal to make $3000 by August 15 to take back to college and last him through the fall semester – around 10 weeks from where he is now. But what could he do? He also knew he'd give his mother the first $500 he earned to help out with groceries and things for his brother and sisters. He is aware that he lives in a 3-bedroom, low-income housing project and that his mom needs both of her jobs to keep the lights on, internet running, and roof over everyone's head.

Fear Force at First: *C'mon James. How're you going to make that much money in one summer? Everyone else is relaxing after a long school year. What makes you think you're capable enough of being hired over more qualified people? You should just relax, there's plenty of Netflix to be watched and videogames to be played...*

Second Base: James was pretty good at basketball. He'd made the team this past year and eventually took over the starting point guard position after an ACL injury to the previous starter. Over his first few days at home, James would look out of his bedroom window and see a group of younger kids playing early in the morning before the high schoolers came and ran them off the court. These younglings didn't look like they knew how to play very well, and James figured they were out there early so no one else could make fun of their game. James had an idea. He quickly drafted a business card online and got 100 cards printed at a local FedEx store. The card looked as follows:

**Ball Out! Summer Basketball Camp with Jay
Clinton Housing Development | Main Basketball Court
Weekdays | 8a-9a | $10 a session
Call (646) 555-0917**

"Impress your friends on and off the court!"

Fear Force at Second: *Really James? You? You didn't even become a starter until the better point guard tore his ACL! Now you want to create a makeshift basketball camp? Those kids are gonna think you're crazy. Where are they going to find $10 to pay you every day? You're wasting your time, James.*

Third Base: The next day, James gets to the court at 7:45am, 15 minutes before the kids would come from the neighboring apartment buildings. James begins shooting free throws, then takes shots from the elbow, then a series of 3-pointers. A few of the kids had arrived and began talking to each other courtside as James continued hoisting shots.

"Did you see that move he did?" said one kid.

"He barely even missed a shot!" said another.

James smiled as he looked over at the slowly growing group of kids. About 10 of them were there now, and he even recognized one of the kids from his church. He motioned for them to come closer.

"Yo, can you teach us to shoot like that?" The kid that James knew walked over, bouncing his ball awkwardly as he came.

"Yeah I got you. And I can show the rest of your friends too."

James spent the next hour going through dribbling drills, proper shooting form, and how to use their legs to power their jump shot. At the end of the hour, the kids were ecstatic. He gave them all his business cards, and even left a few on a nearby bench, knowing that some of the high schoolers would come out to play soon. Within a day, James got 5 out of 10 calls, all from mothers both concerned and elated.

"Is this basketball thing real?" one mother asked.

"I would LOVE for you to coach my son! He's always getting picked on at school and this would help him with his confidence. How much for the month?"

"Well for 4 weeks at $50 a week, that would be $200."

"Count Trevor in," the eager mom continued. "I'll be watching the court on my way out for work in the mornings, so I'll know if you're coaching and not just fooling around. Do you take PayPal?"

Over the next two months, James would make $4400 as 11 kids would sign up for his makeshift morning basketball camp. 11 kids. $50 a week. 8 weeks. $4400. All this for only one hour a day, five days a week. He would give his mother $500 after the first month to help out with groceries and bills for the remainder of the summer – a welcome addition to her paycheck-to-paycheck cashflow.

Fear Force at Third: *Oh James. What makes you think that these kids are going to stay with you throughout the whole summer? At some point, your shot's going to fall off and they won't see you as a coach anymore, but a fraud. You'll be the biggest fraud on the block, and you'll be the laughing stock of the entire housing project. That money's going to leave your pocket just as fast as it arrives anyway...*

Home Plate: It's now the middle of August and James has $3700 to take back with him - $700 more than his projected goal. He also cut down on some of the muscle he gained in the weight room – a price to pay for all the burned calories of morning basketball. After giving $500 to his mother, he gave each of his siblings $100 to use as they saw fit – just not all on ice cream and toys. He taught them the value of a dollar and how to utilize some of their talents beyond the lemonade stand when they get a little older than eight and five. James also realizes he can start a similar business in college to help unskilled players build their confidence.

Not a bad way to complete the Knowledge Cycle, and all without having to find extra work.

Fear Force at Home: *This was a lot of work! All those kids fighting for the ball, and you have to find a way to keep their attention for an entire hour! You won't be able to replicate this in college at all. No student in their right mind is going to pay you to teach them to play. This was the best that you could do, James. It won't get much better than this, so quit while you're ahead.*

Imagine if all James decided to do over the summer was sulk at the limited job openings on the market. What if all he did was curse the economy along with the government that runs it? What if James just complained and never took any initiative?

What if he never invested a small portion of his daycheck into a creative income opportunity? He would be heading back to college the same way he arrived home – with a couple hundred dollars in his pocket and some empty dreams and ideas. Sometimes it's sheer will that moves you from home plate to first base. It's the belief that your presence in the moment has merit. That the contributions you make and conversations you have with yourself matter.

It is important to be aware of the Knowledge Cycle in all areas of our life. Many people have bought into the idea that they'll never have another base to run to. Their lives are lived from chaos to chaos. Every day is filled with more problems than solutions and before they know it, their daycheck has vanished into a vault of high priority fires that all need extinguishing. It's always someone else's fault. The Fear Force at First does a fabulous job of keeping you in your head, and if you keep listening, you'll never get a base hit. We've seen some sample stories from people like James, but what about you?

For instance, you could be strapped for cash and caught up in the "rich get richer while poor get poorer" narrative. Most people that say this have not taken the time to ask themselves *why* they are/feel poor, for that matter. They will hear about ways to grow their money – retail arbitrage, the stock market, low cost mutual funds, real estate investing, etc. – but won't take the first step to see how it works. "One day," they keep telling themselves, but it's just another way to kick the proverbial pebble down the road.

Never forget that when you're called up to bat, you'll think that you're up against the world but you're really playing against yourself. Every batter that's called up in your story is YOU and always will be you. Stop trying to get people to pinch hit for you. Stop glossing over opportunities because it appears tough or you don't think you're capable enough. You cannot create proxies for your progress. It has to be you.

Once you understand that you're capable enough, you'll get your first base hit, then doubles, then triples, and eventually, home runs. The beautiful thing about the Knowledge Cycle is that you can be omnipresent – being on various bases in different scenarios. Just keep rounding the bases. Don't give in to the Fear Forces, or you'll never reach your destination or goals. Like Mike Trout, you have to come ready to play. You have to plug out from the dugout and prepare for the pitch. And to prepare for the pitch, you have to dream. Big. Or your cubicle can become your crucible. Awareness. Acquisition. Affirmation. Audit. Ask questions. Find answers. Do. Review.

GPS AND NAVIGATION

As you work to hit for the cycle, program these bases into your life's GPS and navigation system. Your GPS tells you where you are, while your navigation system tells you where you're headed. Some people are operating on broken navigation systems because they've downloaded the noise of everyone else's opinions of their story. Every time they try to leave drama, their system redirects them back to it. Where in your life is your GPS telling you that you are? Where is your navigation system telling you that you need to go next? Wherever you are in your story, at some point your navigation system has no choice but to direct you towards the desert.

5 | THE DESERT

"In solitude we don't reject the world but have the space to think our thoughts." -Sherry Turkle

One humid August day in 2005, I waved goodbye to my sister and bedroom, and left my apartment for college. My parents accompanied me on an excruciatingly long Greyhound bus ride from New York - all three of us deep in sleep as the bus chewed up the I-80 west for over 12 hours.

I was leaving home and everything I knew of myself for a small university in Southwest Michigan where the ratio of trees to buildings are completely reversed.

As we ventured further and further away from the breakneck cadency of the east, I saw my desert begin to take shape. It took the shape of well-manicured farmlands and industrial factories. It took the shape of cow manure and 3rd floor dormitories. I walked towards my new residence to a small sign on a door that said, *"Ben and Elroy's Room."* Southwest Michigan was more than 700 miles from home. And with all of its siloed glory, it was exactly what I would need for the next seven years.

There has to be some point in your story where a call for something greater happens, and you must leave home. Everything you know and believe you are needs to be left behind for some time in order for you to grow. And this growth happens in a desolate space where your culture is challenged and loved ones' opinions are limited. This is the space that I call the desert. And this is the place towards which you need to escape.

Luke Skywalker would've remained on Tatooine if he didn't receive a prompting from Obi-Wan to join a cause greater than his current situation. He was surrounded by endless miles of desert and limiting beliefs. That was, until the death of his aunt and uncle. With no family left to turn to or home-based excuses to lean on, Luke leaves the planet. Sometimes it takes a sudden *One Day* to wake you up and spring you into action. That *One Day* buys you a first-class ticket into the desert (or in Luke's case, away from it). When your story comes to a crossroads, it's time for you to get away. And not necessarily to another planet.

Disney's favorite lion cub Simba learns a similar lesson. The death of someone he loves (along with his own death sentence) sends all four of his paws scampering off into the desert. In his desert experience, a meerkat and warthog befriend him, tell him not to worry, and shift his diet from savory to "slimy, yet satisfying". There are times when your desert will suck, and everything feels bland, bleak, and all the familiar voices - the ones that both love you for who you are and also don't ever want you to change - become faint during your desert experience. The struggle is inevitable, the strain is real. But we must feel strain before we can feel strength.

So far, we've learned that in this world of 24-hour news cycles, distractions, demands, and high-expectation relationships, there's a very good chance that we're lost within our own stories. We've learned what stories are made of and how they progress. We've learned how to guard our time and the value of where we invest our minutes. We've learned about the cycles in our story and how and why we need to keep them going. And with all of this info, it's time for the long trek to third base. It's time to go forth into the desert and be brave.

BRAVING THE WILDERNESS

Our deserts, as it were, are a form of *wilderness.* The dictionary calls the wilderness «an uncultivated, uninhabited, and inhospitable region." It's that liminal space between our before and after pictures - the places where we lose friends, loved ones, and face turbulent chapters in our story. This is how you grow, learn about yourself, find yourself. This is how you belong.

In her book "Braving the Wilderness," Brene Brown talks about what it takes to find yourself and truly belong: "True belonging has no bunkers. We have to step out from behind the barricades of self-preservation and brave the wild."

It's the self-preservation that blocks us from advancing our narratives. That preservation is a parasite that latches onto progress. It strips away any attempt at making yourself a better person. It blots out all the goals and dreams on new pages of your story until you're left with whatever was most comfortable. Sometimes, the things that give us the most comfort equally provide the most damage.

FORTRESS OF SOLITUDE

No matter how you slice it, there are times where you will need to be alone. In 2016, Paul Jun wrote an article for 99u on the skills one needs when working alone, and how solitude forces you to deal with yourself and get stuff done. According to his article, it seems like being alone causes us to deal with our mishaps and bad experiences. But we can't ignore our flaws forever. Jun further states that it's easy to be distracted from thinking about ourselves in a social setting as we're often wondering about the thoughts of others. But being alone increases the volume of the voices we're trying to keep silent.

In some way, I believe many of us are afraid of those voices. We mute them because if we don't, they'll remind us that we've spent too much time in the same location, doing the same things, with the same people. They will tell us the truth, and the truth pushes people to action. The truth faces Uncle Scar. The truth takes on death stars. And after we spend enough time in our desert, we become more in tune with our truth.

GOING ON VACATION

Banff National Park is located in the Rocky Mountains in the province of Alberta. For those of you who are wondering if this is a real place, it's in western Canada. And for those of you who are wondering if *Canada* is a real place, then I can't help you much further! It is one of the most beautiful places in North America, spanning over 2500 miles of mountainous terrain.

I remember taking my wife back to Banff in 2018 where I proposed six years prior one chilly December day. This time it was around Memorial Day weekend, with the weather projected to be much improved from the chilly December day when I signed my single life away in a steadily climbing gondola. My first trip to Banff was also with my in-laws who lived in Edmonton at the time. As surreal as the snow-capped vistas were,

I knew I had to return with my wife Meika to do things at the pace we wanted to, which, if I was being honest, was really at my pace!

So there we were, back in Banff several years later, with a few days to hike around Lake Louise, Lake Moraine, Johnston Canyon, and relive the 8-min gondola ride up towards the heavens, better known as Sulphur Mountain. THIS to me was vacation. No need for my phone buzzing off the hook with random requests and notifications. No phantom throbbing in the back of my head reminding me of something I forgot to do at home. I was away, and free to face one of the most beautiful expanses of God's creation I had ever seen. Us humans are funny creatures. When we are in our work, we will fill up many moments with noise to avoid the awkwardness of silence. But when we are in our wonder, we cherish the silence. We listen to the rustling of the trees in the woods, the majesty of the waves and the horizon line, and are rendered speechless by starry night skies.

We will pay thousands of dollars a year for the desert or wilderness experience, and in some cases, millions. One Colorado couple on HGTV's *House Hunters* were at the advent of their empty-nester phase and were looking for MORE space! With a budget of over a million dollars, the wife wanted acreage for horses to run amok, and the husband wanted solitude and silence. She wanted more neighs and he wanted less neighbors. In the end, they got a hybrid of both – tons of acreage and quiet for them and visiting family members to enjoy.

Somewhere, deep down, we want to get away and be awed by something bigger and greater than us. We want to be moved by a mission that outlives our life spans to be convinced that something greater than our existence is at work. It reminds us that our existence matters, and that while we're here, we must make the most out of our stories. We must *live* our stories, and not let our stories live us.

You may be in a season of your story where you can't get away. There are too many people and variables that demand your energy and attention, and even one step towards the desert feels like a betrayal to friends and family. They love your presence, your availability, your yeses. But how many yeses do you have left in the account of your heart to give? Is your capacity to give in the black or the red? For many of you, it's been red for a long time.

THE ASSESSMENT

Ok, I know this desert and wilderness stuff sounds like a lot so far, but I really need you to use your head and your ears in this moment for some clarity. This is a pivotal part of your story – *One Day* has shown up and it's not going away any time soon. I need you to use your head and make an assessment of the current chapter of your story. What has been repeatedly occurring in your narrative that you can't seem to shake? What villain has been buying up all the prime real estate on both sides of your brain? In this assessment I need you to do three things:

1. **Stop spending so much time trying to figure out others' thoughts.** You won't know what everyone is thinking and for our sakes, that's a good thing. As one pastor named Steven Furtick once put it, "Stop drawing thought bubbles over other people's heads." Veronica Roth penned it perfectly in the second book of the Divergent Trilogy, *Insurgent.* She said, "People, I have discovered are layers and layers of secrets. You believe you know them, that you understand them, but their motives are always hidden from you, buried in their own hearts. You will never know them, but sometimes you decide to trust them."

2. **Forgive yourself for allowing others to dictate your character.** Usually when we're frustrated and upset, we erupt all over social media, in text messages, or in whoever's ear is willing to listen. Someone has hurt us, and we want the world to know. But if we continue to move at the pace of our hurt without the power of forgiveness, we don't create space to heal, grow, and start a clean chapter. When you forgive yourself, you give yourself a second chance to continue your chapter in a different way. Are you always in a state of frustration because of what someone has done? Forgive them, but that's a nearly impossible task if you also don't forgive yourself.

3. **Learn to control your emotions.** This has major import, because emotions are often the fuel that powers human relationships. The stoics mastered the art of emotional control, and over time they learned how to not respond in every situation out of their emotions, but rather, their principles. People that practice stoicism are usually considered boring, but what they often understand is that every high moment will not last forever. And neither will every low. I'm not saying that you have to walk around like an emotionless brute, but you should understand that not every situation deserves your emotional reaction. The more you control your emotions, the more leverage you have over your reactions. The more leverage you have over your reactions, the less power other people and situations have over you.

THE THREE LEVELS OF LISTENING

I just asked for you to use your head for a moment to make an assessment, and now I'm going to ask for your ears. This will only work if you've taken the time to prepare for your desert experience. You'll need a few moments to yourself so if possible, try to avoid the phone, the spouse, the television, and the kids for a little bit and listen. Find a quiet space and listen as deeply and intently as you can to three things:

1. **Your Heart.** Have you ever listened to your heart before? The rhythmic *ba-bum, ba-bum, ba-bum* of blood pulsing through your left and right ventricles? As joyous as the sound of life sounds, listen a little deeper. *Ba-bum.* What is your heart telling you? *Ba-bum.* What has your heart desired for such a long time that you haven't been able to fulfill? *Ba-bum.* What does your heart need more than anything in this current chapter of your life? Listen to the intricate and intimate spaces of your heart. And find out if both you and your heart are in sync.

2. **Your Home.** Now you can extend your ear from what's going on inside you to what's happening right outside. What does your home sound like? Is it yelling from the spouse or the kids? Reruns of Friends or The Fresh Prince? Does it sound like peace or a cacophony of chaotic compounds? A lot of what's happening in your heart is connected to what's happening in your home. If your heart is in crisis, your home will be affected and vice versa.

3. **Your Habitat.** I ask for your ears a final time to venture a little further out of your dwelling space. While the heart speaks to what's happening within, and the home indicates what's happening without, your habitat encapsulates the others like a Matryoshka doll. What does it sound like right outside your home? What is the pulse of the community and neighborhood? Does it sound like honking rideshare drivers? How about HOA or townhall meetings? Or even squirrels and

cicadas? Listening to the sounds of your habitat will let you know if the spaces you're in are meant for you to stay for a long time or a season. Sometimes we stay in our habitats for too long. The weather changes, and we never migrate or hibernate. And each year, we trick ourselves into believing that we're adding value to the habitat, when we're really not making room for anything that calls us to move beyond our comfort zone.

Look at the three levels of listening as if they're three tracks on your desert album. No one's album is going to sound the same, because everyone's in a different place and time within their story. Remember your supporting cast members and how they all play the main characters in their own story. They all at some point must go through the desert.

But now it's your turn.

THE 40-DAY DESERT RETREAT

THIS is one of the most important parts of this book. I'll encourage you to read straight through it, and then at some point, mentally prepare yourself for this moment. This is where friends and family may get mad. This is the moment where you take your second foot out of the *before* picture and hang out in the liminal space. You are getting ready to shatter the old image of yourself. You are preparing to break a lot of expectations, because this is the only way you can learn and sharpen the tools needed to defeat your villain. The desert awaits you.

There is a life that you want so bad. You dream of it every day, and it's waiting for you to meet it. Every day, it pierces you in the side of your child-like mind, asking you if you're satisfied with your current situation. This life calls to you in the middle of your morning shower, or a sales presentation, or while you're getting chewed up by your boss for being three minutes late.

The life that you're looking for – the purpose that's tailor-made for you to fulfill lies on the other side of the desert. Or, it can be right where you are, and you can only decipher the details in the desert.

You may have dreams of living in Thailand for a year, or finding long lost relatives in Western Africa, or taking a weeks-long photography trip up the Pacific Coastal Highway. You may want to become a world class Poker player, or be fluent in Spanish, or tryout for the NBA. The New York Times may be waiting for your next essay, or Bill Gates may want your thoughts on the future of tech and philanthropy. Whatever your dream is, it's calling. And if you're ready – if you're truly ready and the stars in your eyes have aligned, it starts with 40 days. Why 40 days? Because it's sufficient enough to spend an adequate amount of time at each base of the Knowledge Cycle.

And, well, a Middle Eastern man named Jesus once spent 40 days fasting in a desert, so I guess that warrants some mention!

DAY 1-10: AWARENESS

We talked about this in the previous chapter, but it needs to be reiterated as you're taking your first steps out into the wild. The first few steps will feel weird because you're introducing new ground into your story. In the summer of 2001, my mother took my sister Samantha and I to her home island of Antigua, an 108-sq mile piece of Caribbean paradise boasting 365 beaches (one for every day of the year they say!). This was an eight-week vacation for me, but for my mother, it was home. We were also going to visit my father, who spends most of his time there amongst the sugar cane and five-minute rain. Antigua was an adjustment for Samantha and me. I remember the first day we got there, and Sam and I walked down the hill where my father lived towards the main road that led into town. In typical New

York fashion, we were dressed to the nines in Nikes, designer jeans, and tees. As we walked down the hill and onto the main road, we could feel the eyes of the neighbors peering out of their windows and were immediately reminded that we were foreigners. By day three, we knew to just wear "house clothes" when we were hanging out in the yard or playing in the yards of our neighbors. *House clothes* were what you wore when you weren't trying to impress anyone. You were home, and it was an unspoken rule that home meant you wear whatever worked – garments well suited for laps around the yard, cistern water, and clothespins that chaperoned wet garments in the wind.

Some of the neighbors didn't mind moving around their yards without shoes. (This wasn't to say that they couldn't afford shoes, but it was just the culture, the unspoken rules again). Barefoot or flip flops, unless you were heading out for an event in town. The first time I tried it, I would've thought I was stepping on shards. My feet weren't calloused enough for the earth – or at least this side of it. After a few weeks of tries and laughs from the neighbors, the barefoot experience became easier. The earth accepted my steps and as I walked, I no longer winced or wailed.

Take a deep breath and step onto the rugged and sandy terrain. Feel the uneasiness of the new space. Allow the feet within your mind to grow accustomed to this unfamiliarity. Have a journal or sheet of paper with you, and at the end of every day write about something you're aware of in your life. Are you aware of what's hurting you? Are you aware of the hurt you've caused? Are you aware of what your purpose might be? Every day, shut out the notifications and write. Write for at least five minutes on everything you're aware of or *feel* aware of. Are you aware of how much time you've wasted, how many investments you've walked away from, or how many friends and family you've pushed away? People only begin to find the answers they're looking for when they start to ask the right questions. Now that you're in the desert, give yourself space and permission to ask them.

As you get closer to Day 10, continue to write. Who's that dream guy or girl? What are the qualities they possess that you're looking for? Are you aware that you're open to looking, or maybe aware that you're emotionally unavailable? What about your job? Are you aware that you've given a nickname to every nook and cranny in your cubicle over the last umpteen years? Do you feel that you've outgrown your capacity to add value in your current workspace? If so, are you aware of what could be next, and what are you going to do about it? It is important that people challenge themselves with reality checks because sometimes that's the only way for them to jumpstart their dreams.

Let's say that at the end of every day you've asked yourself five questions connected to your levels of awareness. By Day 10, you should have 50 questions that reflect who you are and what you're aware of. You should start to see patterns in your awareness and where some strengths and weaknesses have taken shape. Has anyone ever told you about these strengths or weaknesses? If these are new for you, then this is good news. The terrain is accepting your feet. The call is growing, the callouses forming. Now that you've gone through a 10-day stretch of "Awareness Q+A," it should set you up for the next 10 days – the days of acquisition.

DAY 11-20: ACQUISITION

If you have a Netflix account, you've probably done your fair share of binge-watching. I'm not really a binger, but I do remember spending the better part of a month watching all nine seasons of *The Office*. Over the years I've had many friends share inside jokes from *The Office* that always left me wondering, *what am I missing out on here? Maybe I should just go find out for myself.* Classic case of FOMO.

Usually when FOMO (Fear of Missing Out) happens, it's based on the idea that other people are having an experience that you're currently not connected to but should be. They're at parties and having fun you want to have. They're speaking in other languages that you can't understand. They're posting engagement photos, and wedding pictures, and having children, and traveling everywhere, and flashing dollar bills, and rescuing Koalas, and the list goes on. What if your FOMO was channeled from a lack of self-reflection? What if all the pondering you did on first base made you aware of an experience you would never want to miss out on, or at least attempt to try? What if your Fear of Missing Out experience was instead connected to your internal well-being, personal growth, mental nourishment, and purpose?

- Fear of Missing Out on loving someone unconditionally

- Fear of Missing Out on paying off your student loans in full

- Fear of Missing Out on forgiving someone who hurt you

- Fear of Missing Out on identifying your gifts

- Fear of Missing Out on mending your marriage

- Fear of Missing Out on investing your time and finances

- Fear of Missing Out on giving back to your community

This list could be endless, but it's there as a reminder of all the other experiences you could be missing out on besides friends doing things you feel you should be a part of. Now, whenever people talk about *The Office,* my acquisition of the entire nine-season storyline gives me much more context. I no longer feel out of the loop, because I immersed myself in the narrative and blocked out any interruptions from the outside world.

For your walk in the sands of days 11-20, I want you to spend time binging on the information you need to connect yourself with the life that you want and what you need to understand in order to get there. People can want to get out of credit card debt, save up money for the honeymoon they never took, quit their job and open a food truck business, but these things don't happen without proper assessment and acquisition. If done in this order, the 10 days of acquisition will help you clear out the white noise that was blocking you from hearing your purpose clearly.

As you're searching for answers to the assessment questions, I want you to ask yourself more questions connected to the information you need. You're going to need the right information and also the right people to help you advance in this part of your story. If you want to lose weight and become fit, read some magazines on fitness and spend time with fit people who've lost weight. Need to increase your credit score? Talk with folks who have a 750-credit score or higher and ask them how they do it. Spend less time with people who spend money every chance they get. Want to become a more positive person? Hang out with more positive people, or those who have learned how to ditch cynicism and learn how they overcame it.

The loyalty of family and friends is well-cherished, but sometimes the cheers from Mom and Dad can only take you so far. Those cheers work well in the beginning of certain seasons.

But there are times when you need to be introduced to new environments and characters – the mysterious and open world that's waiting for you beyond the edge of the forest.

DAY 21-30: APPLICATION

Nine. Nineteen. Five. That was the combination of the first lock I ever owned – well, co-owned to be exact. Juan was my 9th grade high school locker mate and bought the lock for us. Nine, nineteen, five. Over and over again for the rest of the school year, I'd apply these three numbers in a few spins and twists, swapping out Biology books for Math, then Math for Social Studies, then Social Studies for English. Nine, nineteen, five. Monday through Friday, the same case to solve.

Then freshman year ended, and Juan had another locker mate for sophomore year and beyond as friendships and bonds solidified past the algorithm that selected us. Juan would also have to learn a new code as he left me the treasure chest key for future use. I would pass the secret on to Terrell, my close friend and new locker mate for the remainder of high school. Nine, nineteen, five. Nine, nineteen five. Nine, nineteen five...

I wish I could tell you that nine, nineteen, five was the access code to all of your life's problems, but it isn't. The books you want to write, the podcast you want to start, the art you want to create – they all have an access code. As you're halfway through your voyage, your code should start to take shape in the middle of your sandy wilderness. Your access code has been inside of you for years - buried deep beneath your daily routine, your fears and insecurities, and the opinions of those you want to please the most.

This is it. You're at your locker now – the one you've been avoiding forever because you're afraid of the power that rests on the other side. This one locker is in the middle of your desert, and it's been calling you. The sound has gotten louder as the voices of your cultures and community have gotten quieter. This is where you take what you've learned and put it to the test. Get the journal and write. Open Microsoft Word and type. Compose the song. DM the social media influencers. Draw the thought. Perform the backflip. Make the slime. Over the next ten days, do, do, do. Whatever nine, nineteen, five looks like for you, unlock that energy over and over again and put it into your dream.

One film project I was involved in started with a 2-year-old boy doodling away on a sheet of paper. For anonymity's sake, we'll call him 'Max.' We had Max sit at a table in a classroom, where his teacher supplied him with a box of Crayola crayons. All we told Max to do was color on the paper while we filmed shots from different angles. Max took a couple colors, swiped back and forth for a few seconds, looked back towards the teacher, and yelled "finished!"

"Thank you, Max," the teacher responded, "but we need you to color just a little bit more."

"Okay."

Max took another color from the crayon box, swiped back and forth for about seven more seconds, looked behind him, and yelled, "I'm finished!"

"Okay, Max. Just one more time, please."

A different color from the box, another seven second scribble, the eventual look back.

"I'm finished!"

I must say that during that time, I really had to applaud Max. This precocious two-year-old powered his way through his challenge in seven seconds or less. He nine-nineteen-fived the mess outta that thing! I admired his courage to use the tools in front of him to create work. In spite of onlookers and critics, he was undaunted. He never hesitated or wondered what we were thinking of him. The kid just colored away, and that was it. He shipped, then shipped again.

But what if you're still afraid of doing? Marketing master Seth Godin speaks on the concept of shipping (getting your work out in the world) and what prevents most people from doing so consistently. In an article for 99u, Adobe's website for creatives and making ideas happen, Seth would refer to us having a lizard brain – that scared voice in our heads that stops us from deploying our work into the world often and on time. Sometimes that lizard takes the form of people that slow your work down via constant suggestions, committees, and status quo-ed thought processes. Somehow, we need to learn to fight this resistance force so we can make more progress in our creative work.

A lizard for Seth, Fear Forces for me. We covered the Fear Forces in depth in the previous chapter, so I'll give the resistance a new name in this chapter. I'll call this resistance, The Evil Jury.

THE EVIL JURY

The Evil Jury is everywhere. In your Twitter feed. At the mall. In your family and friends' groups. It seems like you can't get away. But you can. Just who is this "Evil Jury" anyway? The Evil Jury is the group of people you think are always out to get you. To talk about how unattractive or worthless you are. Or how much you suck at shooting free throws or putting on makeup. Or how you'll never be good enough to be in the "in" group (does that still exist?). They hide in the audible whispers of those who are in the same room but aren't directing their intimacies towards you. They grow hot and rise up into your cheeks at the worst possible time. They tell you that you can't sing. That your speaking delivery is horrible. That the boy who took your number is never going to call you. That the girl you poured your soul out to is never going to text you back.

Why do we allow the Evil Jury to exist? Why give them strength by believing the nothingness? The Evil Jury's number one motive is to make you doubt yourself. And if you've been doubting yourself for a long time in any area, then here are a couple things you need to understand.

1. **The Evil Jury uses doubt as its oxygen.** What are you currently doubting yourself in? Are you trying to change a career but are waiting on the validation from someone you revere? Stop giving doubt residence in your mind and the Evil Jury will subside.

2. **The Evil Jury has no intentions of keeping you happy.** In her book *Year of Yes*, television producer, director, and film writer Shonda Rhimes illustrates the importance of being around happy people:

Happy whole people are drawn to happy whole people. But nothing makes a toxic person more miserable and destructive than a happy whole person. Unhappy people do not like it when a fellow unhappy person becomes happy. I am absolutely sure that this is true, because I used to be an unhappy person.

Do not allow yourself to buckle under the weight of other people's insecurities or unhappiness. It's the mosquito bite from the Evil Jury and it will itch like hell. Find your happy place in the desert, and if you can't find one, make one up until it becomes a reality. You can beat your Evil Jury by realizing that words and thoughts carry weight only if you give them permission to. Destroy the Evil Jury by acknowledging your awesomeness and that you have places to go and people to add value to.

As you go through Days 21-30, write down what you were able to accomplish for the day. Even if you tried and failed or didn't try at all, write it down and pen a new set of questions connected to your actions. Did you set out to accomplish what you needed to do? If not, then what stopped you? Did you leave your desert too early? Why, who, or what called you out of it? Maintain the solitude. Keep asking the questions and writing the answers. Keep doing, without fear or recompense until you reach Day 30.

By Day 30, you should start to see more patterns. Patterns that point not to who you need to be, but what you need to do. Sometimes we think it's everyone around us that needs to change and get their lives together when it's really us. What if *you're* the one who's causing all the problems in your heart, home, and habitat? What if *you* are the member of your own Evil Jury, better yet, someone else's? Somewhere, these patterns should be leading you towards your purpose. If you haven't caught a glimpse of your purpose yet, you'll need to spend some more days at each phase – asking more questions and doing the work to find the answers. Without a proper stretch of assessments, acquisitions, and applications, you won't properly prepare for the final stretch of the desert – the audit.

DAY 31-40: AUDIT

By now, your face and feet are matted with sand. You've screamed out into the middle of nowhere and it's been rough and uncomfortable. There's no one at this point to walk alongside you and tell you how amazing you are. But that's ok, because your locker should be open by now. You should have found your nine, nineteen, five. In this final 10-day stretch, you're going to wrestle with whatever you found on the other side of your locker. Your audit is the newly discovered truth you speak to yourself, no matter what it takes or costs. This is the truth you'll take with you out of the desert, and the truth you'll need to defeat your villain.

It took Simba a while to realize Scar was his villain. He had spent a good amount of time splashing in waters and slurping worms. But his childhood friend Nala came back and reminded him of his purpose. He was away from home for too long and he learned what needed to be learned in the desert. Let's be fair though – it did also take a nudge from a wise baboon to both realign and remind him of who he was. Simba had to take his place in the circle of life. And now you must too.

Workouts are meant to be intense. They're meant to put your muscles and mind under enormous pressure and resistance. Workouts break your muscles down so they can rest and return stronger than before. But right at the end of your workout is a cooldown phase. This is where you take the time to breathe and get your heartrate back down to a normal pace. The audit is the cooldown. As you cool down in Days 31-40, ask yourself questions reflecting on the work you did in the previous 30. Did you find your purpose? Did you discover your path? What did you learn about your days in the desert? How were you stretched in a way that was different from your usual? Make your pages your therapist as you begin to see a new vision come to fruition. The lack of distractions should have created a nesting place for your dreams to take shape.

As you meander through your audit, figure out how you've grown and what's needed of you for your journey home. Because at this point you should've received new instructions. New commandments. A new way of living that will either confuse or liberate those who are at the end of your return. Sometimes home will have shifted and will not be the location you left. Sometimes home will be what's ahead - a new terrain to try, another dwelling place far different from what was left behind.

For those of you who are back "home", and someone has left you for the desert, it might feel like a betrayal. When people are part of our routines, they also become part of our ecosystem. They are indelible notes on the songs in our heart, home, and habitat. "How dare they leave?" we ask ourselves, unaware of the new notes they need to listen to. We become angry and possessive and want our loved ones in every chapter of our story. But life doesn't work that way. There will be times when we need to celebrate people's exodus from our lives. The marriage. The graduation. The breakup. Their exit gives us healthy doses of reality - like the last family member or friend to leave the party. Sometimes, their march towards the desert is a blessing in disguise because it creates the necessary room for both you and them to grow.

And just like that, your 40 days in the desert are up. And just like that, it's about to go down.

6 | DISCOVERING YOUR MISSION

"There's no external reward that's more fulfilling than being in service to the world." – Kyle Cease

I sat on the couch with bated breath. I was glued to the fibers by some wild combination of fanaticism and religion. It had been weeks of preachy pundits pontificating prospects that would be a good fit for my team. I read and watched countless articles and videos about where certain players would fall when it was time for us to pick. All of my research was just frantic swipes in the dark, hoping that this was the year the light would come on. The pick was in. The commissioner approached the podium.

"With the 4th pick, in the 2015 NBA draft, the New York Knicks select... Kristaps Porzingis!"

What!?!?!? You've gotta be kidding me! Who on earth is that? How did I miss watching his highlights on YouTube? I was flabbergasted along with the majority of the Knick fans attending the event. The young Latvian smiled as he walked up to the stage to shake the commissioner's hand. He was lanky but carried a calm confidence. A bevy of boos rose from the crowd. A young fan with blue glasses flashed across the screen, grabbing his head and phone in disbelief. A wave of despair came across New York for a few moments, and it looked like the Knicks' season was ending before it had even started. After the ceremonial handshake and pics with the commissioner, Porzingis shared his thoughts about the boos he heard when his name was called.

"I have to do everything that's in my hands to turn those booing fans into clapping hands."

From the previous 23 Euro-Asian players that were drafted as NBA lottery picks, the only players that mounted to be All-Stars were Dirk Nowitzki, Pau Gasol, and Yao Ming. So, when the Knicks selected a 7 ft 3, 230-pound Latvian center to round out their roster, there wasn't a lot of enthusiasm. Porzingis was a skinny unknown. His stock value was extremely low, even though he had high upside and a high ranking on some draft boards. But as November came and Porzingis began to perform, he started to wow the crowd with high-octane blocks, threes, and put-back dunks. Long story short, the New-York-style boos turned to cheers as Porzingis set team rookie records. Kevin Durant called him a "unicorn." And then he got injured. And then in March of 2019, in pure Knicks fashion, Kristaps Porzingis was traded to the Dallas Mavericks for players and draft picks. Not a bad ROI for a skinny teenager from Latvia who was booed on his draft night.

Let's imagine for a moment that Porzingis was a privately held company who on draft night was preparing for his initial public offering, or IPO. As he declared for the draft, he would go public under the ticker name PZGS at $15 a share. This would be an extremely low valuation for someone who was drafted 4th out of 60 players. As more tape was made available from his play during the 2015 Vegas Summer League, his stock would rise to $20. Porzingis would finish his rookie year with his stock value around $30. It would more than double in price to $65 a share (let's say, all-star valuation prices) before he had a season-ending injury that kept him out of play for over a year. By the time he was traded to Dallas, his stock would be around $60 a share, his age still young, his body still developing, and his value quadrupling since his draft nearly 4 years prior. Like Kristaps, we are all on a mission - to use the moments given to us to add value in the places we're in, even if it's for a few seasons.

WE ARE ALL STOCKS

Whether you like it or not, we are constantly under valuation and evaluation. People are trying to determine if we're trustworthy enough, capable enough, and committed enough – all falling within their latitude of value. The more we show up for someone, make them smile, support their cause, and catch their tears, our value goes up in their minds and hearts. In some cases, the more we perform for people, the more we're considered their friend – someone they can go to when they need help or support. Our character is out there on the market, and based on what you're currently doing, people are buying or selling you.

In 2008 when the market crashed and burned, stocks were pretty much on sale. I wouldn't have known this if my friend Jamarious hadn't come bursting into my room one junior year during college. He told me to sign up for a Sharebuilder account and check out some stocks. I was close to broke, but I obliged and bought one share of Wells Fargo (which at the time was at a single-digit stock price). Over the next several months, I would watch Wells Fargo go up in price by about $10, and of course my investing naiveté wouldn't allow me to keep my earnings in the market for much longer. I cashed out and bought God knows what shortly after the money transferred into my bank account. Sometimes we give up on projects and people right in the middle of their growth season, not realizing we're building walls between ourselves and our blessings.

I'm no financial guru, but to me, a stock in layman's terms is a piece of a publicly traded company. When you buy shares of stock, you're buying a piece of that company, instantly making you a shareholder. Before these companies are stocks, they usually have to determine what their value is after a series of funding rounds from wealthy financiers. When you find yourself in the desert, you're also supposed to find your mission. And when you find your mission, you will need support from an angel investor.

ANGEL INVESTORS

Today's parent has immense pressure to be the best parent ever. I believe that not only do they have to make sure their child feels loved, cared for, and protected, but also remind the rest of the world of their child's existence through social media. This is the zeitgeist, where a parent's success can at times feel synonymous with their children's accomplishments. It's a never-ending venture – to instill confidence, wonder, and security within the child while at the same time trying to secure those same treasures for themselves.

Enter my mother, Eve. She is creative, crazy, and one of the most amazing people I know. (I know, everyone says this about their mother, but allow me some braggadocio)! She's got that spicy Caribbean grit – hot feet, sharp tongue, open hands, soft heart. Growing up, she made me feel like I could be or do anything, and then would do everything in her power to let the world know how amazing I was. At times it was really embarrassing as she would wax on about my talent or potential to people whose ears were ready to turn the channel. I was so ready for the public beaming to be over, but she didn't care. I was her son, her firstborn. She was my mother and my very first angel investor.

Angel investors are the ones that believe in you when others belittle you. They are the first to believe in your story – your book beyond its cover. They are first in line to hear your dreams and first to encourage you to chase them. And when your dreams come true, they are right there, the first to celebrate. Angel investors are your first 'yeses' in a sea of a thousand 'nos.' They will always believe more in the reward than the risk.

It's a cruel world out there where people are spilling toxic substances all across the pages of your story. It seems like each chapter of your narrative has a new challenge designed to have you rise to another level. Sometimes all we're looking for is someone to be a safe space *for* us and believe *in* us. We want someone to laugh with us when everyone else is laughing at us. We desire a person who doesn't want our dreams to fall below cloud nine. We crave a listening ear, a soft shoulder, and a warm heart.

For Porzingis, a player scout for the Knicks named Clarence Gaines was his angel investor. Sports teams rely on scouts to evaluate talent and see if they're a good fit for their organization come draft day. While other NBA teams were focused on scouting home-grown players at the Division-1 level, Gaines convinced then team president Phil Jackson that Porzingis would be a good player to invest in. Had it not been for Clarence Gaines, Porzingis would not have been as high on the Knicks radar and would not have gotten a chance to prove his value. Whenever the time comes around for you to present your value, show up and confirm your angel investors' faith in you. And like Porzingis, you must have the ability to be better than other people's scouting reports of you.

FIVE QUESTIONS AND SAYINGS WE NEVER OUTGROW FROM CHILDHOOD

As our first angel investors usually are our parents, they're the first to believe in our mission. From what you've already read by now, there are times where we lose that mission or never knew what our mission was to begin with. From early childhood, we try to make sense of our own existence, and we validate that existence through five questions or statements, each of which we never outgrow. Even though you're out of the desert, the real journey is only just beginning. Here are five questions and statements we start using in our childhood that often follow us into our adulthood:

1. **Are you my friend?** "Hi best friend!" Growing up, my sister often said this whenever she saw her partner-in-crime. It was a way of acknowledging the depth of her relationship with that person. It was an external response to an internal inquiry, "Are you my friend?" Social media has changed the meaning of the term *friend*, which in essence means a person whom you have affinity or affection for. When we internalize this question, we're secretly asking others, "Are you in my corner? Do we have affinity over certain things, ideas, people, or experiences? Can I count on you when I need you?" And we always expect the best. The reality is, we're always disappointed when people don't support us, have time for us, or have affinity with what we believe. Our expectations for our friends are extremely high in this era, where we're often feeling overwhelmed and need more support in our story. *Fake friends* start to creep into our minds when they disappoint us, which keeps us tumbling in a vicious cycle of unmet expectations. As you grow in your mission, you'll be asking this within your mind many times and will encounter oth-

ers who'll do the same. One way to deal with this is by lowering your expectations from others, while increasing expectations from yourself. You might be mad that Daisy missed out on your graduation, but don't allow Daisy's absence to hijack your state of mind. Remember, Daisy's a character in her own story too.

2. **Is this ok?** After we find out if we have affinity with the person, we want to know how far it's safe to go. This is the old "child-touching-the-stove" story. Or wanting to stay by your best friend after school. We often ask our parents for permission to do things at an early age (*Can I have another cookie?*) and hope that they say "yes." We're constantly checking for boundaries and that doesn't change as we get older. We desire safety within our spaces and relationships and when we don't feel safe, we create boundaries. If we ask if it's ok, and we feel like it's not, we draw back into ourselves, unfollow and unfriend people, and retreat into our thoughts and private spaces. This is the question you asked yourself before you went into the desert. The desert breaks the idea of who you believe you are, which is usually in a place you consider safe. Sometimes, it *is* ok. Sometimes we must take the leap of faith, even when the person isn't our friend and allow different ink to fall on the pages of our story.

3. **Can you help me?** First, we find affinity. Next, we check for the boundaries. And then, when we know the boundaries of our own abilities, we ask for help. Children want to be picked up when they can't walk, are too tired, or just need love. They want assistance early and often. We do the same when we have our own children, get kicked out of our homes, or crumble under the weight of student loans. Children know that they can't go through life by themselves and need help.

And many of us find it hard to complete our tasks and missions by ourselves as well. Sometimes the help is necessary, while other times we have to "figure it out on our own." That's what our parents sometimes told us when we had 2nd grade math homework, and that's what we at times have to tell ourselves. *If no one's going to help me, I'll figure it out on my own. (Cue the story of The Little Red Hen).* We can't always get angry at the world when they don't help us. We have to learn to cope and discover the strength already instilled in us to get the job done. Or watch a few YouTube videos!

4. **Look what I'm doing/Look what I did!** My nieces went through a phase where whenever they saw me, they both had to show me the latest thing they'd learned. "Look at this, Uncle Elroy! Look what I can do!" They were 3 and 7 at the time, and they would somersault, or twirl really fast, or high kick, or do whatever was the latest "cool kid" dance at the time. This told me that they wanted me to acknowledge their existence and that they learned new things since the last time I saw them. They needed the affirmation of knowing what they're doing can be observed, cheered, and celebrated. As we get older, we say the same things in our social feeds. *Look where I traveled! Look what I ate! Look who I ran into! Look what I just did!* We want the world to know that we exist. And that we're moving, doing, and experiencing things that should matter.

5. **How did I do?** First, we establish the relationship. Next comes the boundaries. Then we need help. Finally, once we've executed, we want to know others' opinions and observations. Children love receiving positive feedback. And I suppose parents love giving it. If you were born into a loving nuclear family, you most likely walked around in a bubble of love and positivity for

the first several years of your life. You could dip your brush in a few paint colors, swipe it across a sheet of paper, and your parents would post it on the fridge for everyone to see. *"Mommy, Daddy, look what I did!"* You'd come home ecstatic with your Piscasso-esque masterpiece, and your parents would smile like it was the greatest work in the world. The issue arrives when you finally enter the world and *How Did I Do?* meets the red pen of the elementary teacher, the fist from the bully, the chuckles from the popular kids, and the blank faces from the church members. No one has the face muscles to smile at your work extensively beyond your early childhood. But we still expect happy feedback from our work, and by now you already know what can happen when we increase our expectations of others. As the years go by, we will continue to put out work, step over our villains, and ask everyone how we did. Just be careful, because extensive asking leads to the creation of *Evil Juries* – all ready to hold up low scorecards in our minds.

All of these questions and statements live at the root of many of our interactions. They've taken place throughout our lives, and now you can pinpoint them and know where they stem from. Here are a few examples:

"You will not believe what happened to me today!" *Are you my friend? Do you have time to listen to my struggle?*

"I need a favor." *Can you help me? Can I depend on you?*

"Who's going to be at the party?" *Is this a safe space? Can I be myself with people I know and trust and not be in my head?*

"I just got invited to speak at this startup event." *Look at what I'm doing! Did you hear what I just said?*

"What did you think of the piece I wrote?" *How did I do? Is my contribution to this world enough? Am I enough?*

When we struggle with the unanswered questions, we purchase a one-way ticket straight to our head. We stay there and allow our inner critic to take over. Our inner critic constantly evaluates all of our friendships and people who come into our space at a rapid pace. Left unchecked, it sabotages hope for other people and yourself, and your inner critic can evolve into your inner cynic.

THE QUESTION WE NEED TO STOP ASKING OUR CHILDREN

One of those unanswered questions is one that lives with us from the time we were children. In spring of 2001, my 8th grade year was coming to an end and the yearbook was being developed. Those working on the project first asked for baby pictures, then school portraits, and finally the million-dollar question:

"What do you want to be when you grow up?"

At the time I had no idea. I knew I liked art and stories, so I put down what I thought was most reasonable at the time and was the only one in my graduating class to have this title under my name.

Cartoonist.

That was the first thing I could think of that made sense to me. So right there, among the pics of Class of 2001 grads aspiring to be rappers, doctors, basketball players, and rich snobs, stood the name "Elroy Byam, Cartoonist." Today, with the change in our economy, there are scores of college-grads in fields that have nothing to do with their degree. An English grad could be on the department store sales floor selling running shoes. An engineering grad may be twirling around in her office chair at a marketing firm. Nothing is as linear as it used to be, and the education-to-economy pipeline is no longer as clear-cut.

"What do you want to be when you grow up?" is a very loaded question. It asks children to identify a light at the end of the tunnel and run as fast as they can towards it. The issue arises when those children come of age and never reach that light – that dream their parents are salivating to share with other inquirers in their semi-surface conversations. *My son's a doctor. My daughter's a lawyer. My grandson works on Wall Street.* Children are forced to digest their aspirations quickly. They learn early on that their identity is celebrated when rooted in a title or position. But what happens when people graduate from college and don't hit that mark? What happens when they don't become what they told their parents they'd be?

We need to shift this question from a being question to a *doing* question. What if we started asking children:

How would you like to serve when you grow up?

This shifts our focus from internal to external. When we don't hit the internal target, we're messed up inside. We didn't end up being what we put down on our yearbooks and now we feel like a failure. But what if our life story was focused on service? What if our story was about finding the best way to add value to humanity? When we focus on how we'd like to serve, we don't connect our lives to any specific title or individual achievement, but rather how we can best help others. Service takes the pressure off of performing and allows us to move from our head to our heart. In other words, it gives us the courage to move from fear to love.

A THIN LINE BETWEEN LOVE AND FEAR

I remember scrolling through Facebook one day and it looked like 80-90 percent of everyone seemed extremely frustrated. Statuses like "I'm cutting this person off" or "Stay away from people who" littered my feed. It seemed like the school of thought was filled with students that felt like they had no authentic connections or real friendships. *"Why is everyone so angry about their relationships with other people?"* I thought to myself. *"Why does it seem like friendship is something that's so hard to do?"* I went and Googled the word *friend*:

Friend /frend/

noun

| a person whom one knows and with whom one has a bond of mutual affection, typically exclusive of sexual or family relations. |

A bond of mutual affection. It appeared as if those that were pouring out their frustration on my timelines were upset at not receiving the equal levels of affection they were sending out. Those bonds had been broken somehow, and the affection was no longer apparent. *Let me look up what affection means,* I thought to myself, and then I googled the term:

Affection /əˈfekSH(ə)n/

noun

| a gentle feeling of fondness or liking. |

I began to put some of the pieces together and had some interesting thoughts. *Could it be that friendship merely meant two people who had a gentle feeling of fondness or liking towards each other? What happened to that kind of feeling?* I looked at the synonyms that rested below *affection's* definition and one of the words stood out more than the others.

Love.

Could friendship really be that clear? Could friendship be just two people that 'love' each other? I started getting excited as I began decoding this friendship mess. I immediately left Google and went to one of the most popular sections of the Bible's New Testament that's often read at weddings, 1 Corinthians 13:

> Love is patient, love is kind. It does not envy, it does not boast, it is not proud. It is not rude, it is not self-seeking, it is not easily angered, it keeps no record of wrongs. Love does not delight in evil but rejoices with the truth. It always protects, always trusts, always hopes, always perseveres. Love never fails...

There it was – the recipe for great friendships and relationships hidden in plain sight. I decided to dig a little deeper. *It seems like everyone is shouting each other out, but they're really afraid to tell others how they feel. Maybe they're afraid in general, trying to maneuver through a world no one prepared them for.* Taking these thoughts, I then did something I'd never done before. I took the word "fear", plugged it in the 1 Corinthians 13 message by changing what was affirmative to negative, and quickly saw a recipe for disaster:

> Fear is impatient, fear is not kind. It is envious, it boasts, and is proud. It is rude, it is self-seeking, it is easily angered, it keeps records of wrongs. Fear delights in evil and is irritated with the truth. It never protects, never trusts, never hopes, never perseveres. Fear always fails.

Whoa. Finally, I felt like I had come to a conclusion. One that many of us have shied away from – hidden deep within betrayals, no-shows, and shards of broken trust. We never asked for it, but here it was – a slow bleed across years of endless newsfeed updates. We have become immensely afraid of each other. We have become people growing in fear, not love:

Fearful people are impatient. They don't make time for people to understand them, nor do they provide grace and space for someone else to grow on them.

Fearful people are not kind. They walk past many people without saying hello or acknowledging their existence, even when those people acknowledge them first.

Fearful people are envious. The comparison and performance culture have led them to not just keep up with the Joneses, but make others forget that the Joneses even exist.

Fearful people are boastful. They must remind you of what they have accumulated or experienced. They find it hard to turn the attention away from themselves.

Fearful people are proud. They will not allow themselves to be seen as lesser than in any situation. Fearful people find it hard to say "I'm sorry" first or even apologize in general.

Fearful people are rude. They do not care whether or not they hurt your feelings and find empathy a hard language to learn.

Fearful people are self-seeking. They look out for themselves first and must make sure their well-being is taken care of. The situation must have a benefit for them as they find it hard to create opportunities for others to have the spotlight.

Fearful people are easily angered. Their fuse is extremely short, and wherever they go, they leave a hoard of eggshells around them.

Fearful people keep records of wrongs. They hold grudges against others at high rates. Their hearts are clogged with receipts from things people have done to them and others both intentionally and inadvertently, often without the other individual knowing the wrong they did.

Fearful people do not celebrate the truth. Not every truth is good news, but it should be a starting point to lead fearful people out of dark unknowns and into brighter futures. When we step into our truth, it liberates us but aggravates those who are in fear.

Fearful people do not protect. They don't take time to think about others' boundaries and how often they violate other people's time, talent, temple, and treasure.

Fearful people do not trust. Their hearts have been broken into unrecognizable parts, and they've put caution tape all around it. Few people are allowed to share in their vulnerability, and even fewer are granted intimacy.

Fearful people do not hope. They feel like they don't have much to look forward to, so they just slosh around in the flotsam and jetsam of a bleak reality. Fearful people don't believe in light at the end of the tunnel, just more darkness.

Fearful people do not persevere. They are inconsistent in tending to things that elevate their life's journey. They are quitters. Fearful people are concerned about anything that will destroy their ecosystem, even if their ecosystem has slowly been destroying them.

These are the ingredients of a fearful person. This is what has been gnawing at the roots of our private and social outbursts. We tend to confidently speak the language of the environment we've spent the most time in, and sometimes that environment is fear. When we live in fear, breathe fear, and respond to everything out of fear, we sentence ourselves. We fail.

All of human behavior stems from either fear or love. The New Testament further states in 1 John that "There is no fear in love. But perfect love drives out fear, because fear has to do with punishment." This was my realization. We have been punishing people for years for how they treated us and broke our expectations. And by doing so, we've been punishing ourselves. This punishment adds zero value to your story. Your story grows when you move from your head to your heart, or from fear to love. That's why falling in love feels so magical. Because what you're really experiencing is falling out of fear. And when we say, "I love you," what we're *really* saying is two things:

1. "I'm not afraid to say that I love you."

2. "I'm not afraid of you."

In a world filled with fearful people, one of the biggest gifts you can give someone is genuinely letting them know that you're not afraid of their presence and existence. Loving people encourages them to take up space in places they were once afraid to be. Ultimately, there is no fear in love. Because whatever we fear, we do not love. And whatever we love, we fear the absence of.

As you discover your mission, you'll need to move forward in serving others. How will you serve when you "grow up?" How will you love? What product, service, or cause will you champion that will change the world and dent the ones around it? You're out of the desert now. Gather your loved-based, service-filled mission and prepare to do the work.

IPO DAY

I remember when I first heard about the company Beyond Meat. My wife and I had finished watching a 2017 documentary on Netflix called *What the Health,* which gave a somewhat biased yet bold perspective on the health and pharmaceutical industry. Suffice it to say that when the credits rolled, my wife was virtually done with meat. A couple days later, she walked into the house with something she said was going to replace her meat intake.

"It's a Beyond Meat Burger. They make it from beets or something like that."

"A Beyond what?" I answered, not caring much about her newfound religion.

Long story short, after having a few bites of the plant-based alternative I was hooked and within a couple months almost completely converted to veganism. *Almost.*

Two years after my first bite, *Beyond Meat* would go public – introducing itself to the stock market under the ticker name BYND and price its IPO at roughly $25 a share. The stock first traded on May 2, 2019 at $46 a share and ended its day at $65.75, a whopping 163% up from its original IPO price. This made Beyond Meat the best-performing IPO since Palm Pilot in 2000. Within six weeks, the stock would rise 550% to nearly $170 a share! In layman's terms, for every share you bought around the opening trade and sold around the six-week mark, you would've made $134 x the number of shares. Talk about profit!

After a series of sharing your vision and ideas with people privately, a day must come when your story goes to market and you emerge from the shadows. Your IPO is the day when the public gets to choose whether or not they want to invest in you. At this point, everything you do will be under intense scrutiny. Those who have bought into whatever you're selling will want to know how the story will progress, while those who haven't invested in you should feel like they're missing out.

QUARTERLY GOALS

When a stock climbs, the shareholders make money. Somewhere, a presentation was made and either sales goals were met or new products, services, and experiences were introduced in a way that excited investors. This usually happens every three months or once a quarter. What if you gave yourself a report card every quarter and checked in on your personal progress? This would be the equivalent of running yourself through the audit part of the knowledge cycle. Remember, the best companies, organizations, and people are the ones who run through the knowledge cycle as often as possible.

Every three months, you should check in on yourself and see if you've delivered on your own promises. Have you started the project or business you said you would? What about the social media page? If so, have you reconnected with your followers and updated them on what's going on? Remember, people are asking themselves why they should invest or continue to invest in you. The winners are those who can sell their vision both consistently and at a high level – the ones who keep you waiting with bated breath for the next page of their story. In other words, people are asking, *"What's next and why should I care?"*

THE 100,000 TICKET PRIZE

The 90s was a great time to be a kid. From *Hook* to *Matilda,* every children's flick seemed to be about kids learning to be independent and getting one over on the adults. There were also wacky toys like Nerf guns, Stretch Armstrong, Pogs, and Polly Pocket. Gameboys, arcades, and lots of laser tag. And being a New Yorker, one of those unforgettable laser tag spots from the 90s was a now-closed midtown hole-in-the-wall called Laser Park.

Laser Park was THE PLACE for second-wave Millennial New Yorkers to celebrate at least one of their elementary birthdays. Besides the quintessential laser tag experience, there was plenty of arcade-like folly ala Dave and Busters style to rack up large amounts of tickets for cool prizes. Usually my Laser Park trips ended up within the 1200-1500 ticket range – enough for tons of candy, finger traps, silly putty, and a multi-colored slinky. These would all be on the bottom rung of the prize section. As your eyes floated higher, you'd see prizes for yo-yos, action figures, video games, and then the mothership of all prizes – the video game console.

Jump back in time with me for a second. The year is 1997, where 9-year-old me sports a Looney Toons tie-dye shirt with high-water jeans. I've just finished playing a couple exhausting rounds of laser tag where I placed nowhere near first but would recoup my loss with fistfuls of tickets from other button-mashing games requiring child-like dexterity. As parents began coming to pick up their kids, it was time to cash out. (Remember, I'm averaging around 1200-1500 in tickets). I look towards the counter to see what I can afford. Candy. Slime. Finger traps. Cheap figurines. I swap my tickets for the trinkets and sigh as I look up at the prize of all prizes. A brand-new Nintendo 64 game console is perched high up on the top shelf like a bald eagle. It's value? Let's say 100,000 tickets!

Who has that much time, effort, and dexterity to play Whack-a-mole and Skee ball for the billionth time? This is the allure of the 100,000-ticket prize. Places like the late Laser Park and Dave and Busters make these prizes so high in ticket value, you have to spend endless amounts of time and money to build up that kind of capital. After a while, most people will just settle for whatever's on the first shelf – the easy to access, edible rewards with no nutritional or monetary value.

Gary Vaynerchuck is the CEO of Vaynermedia and more commonly known to online audiences as GaryVee. It's no secret that Gary wants to buy the New York Jets franchise. In his mind, the Jets are his 100,000-ticket prize. He always talks about the game of *trying* to buy the Jets more than actually buying them, which he says he'll most likely accomplish in his 60s. At the prize station, Gary could purchase whatever he wants, but he keeps his eyes focused on the green team at the top shelf – the prize with the ticket price that would make a lottery winner blush.

What's your 100,000-ticket prize? What keeps you putting one foot in front of the other in spite of the trials, temptations, and terrain? If you don't have a prize of high-value in your vision, make room for one. Those that don't make room continue to be ok with whatever the ticket prizes are on the lowest shelf. These shelves are priced to keep you satisfied enough to spend your lot and return another day to do the same. Your 100,000-ticket prize should make people think you're insane, only for you to have the last laugh when you eventually pluck the prize from its perch. THIS is the oil that keeps your engine running. THIS is the true discovery of your mission.

DISCOVERING YOUR MISSION

By now, I hope that you have at least a glimpse into who you are or are trying to become. You should have an understanding that the world works best when we willingly pour our best selves back into it. But we also need both time and space to develop and evolve into our best selves. The world is waiting on you to free yourself from your Evil Jury and muster up the courage to defeat your villain.

Your villain could be anything. It could be shaped like a man, woman, or a 40oz bottle. It could be on your DVR filled with hours of reruns of your favorite show or nestled deep within the walls of your hippocampus. And unfortunately, your villain could also be in the form of someone you spend a lot of time with! By now you should know your villain well, but you may not always recognize them. All things considered, your mission is to defeat your villain and save the world by *serving* the world. Your greatest weapon against your villain is the knowledge of yourself. Villains take advantage of people who don't know themselves. When you don't know yourself, you don't respect yourself. And when you don't respect yourself, you aid your villain.

You are too close now. You have found yourself, your vision, and your stock has gone public. People have invested in your vision – one that should be so courageously big that it amuses insecure people. As your story progresses, check in on yourself often along with those who've invested in you. Keep your investors interested by bravely leading the charge in your vision. And most importantly, keep a "diversified portfolio." This is the best way to stay emotionally balanced and prepared for any random "One Days" that show up in your story. Sometimes, we invest too much of our time and heart into one stock, one person, or one experience. When they fail us, we feel the full weight of the loss because we were hoping for continued growth and profit from their presence and contribution.

California pastor Erwin McManus shared his thoughts on what a psychological diversified portfolio looks like on Lewis Howes' podcast, The School of Greatness:

> I'm going to focus my life on loving people. I'm going to focus my life on giving people hope. I'm going to focus my life on helping other people find meaning, and I'm going to find my meaning in serving others, not in having others serve me, then you'd actually diversified... A lot of us don't have a psychological diversified portfolio. Our whole lives are about ourselves. And the way I look at it is that every day of my life someone is doing well. Every day of my life, someone I love is moving forward. Every day of my life, someone I love is doing something awesome. And so there isn't a day in my life that there isn't something to celebrate because it's not all about me.

Discovering your mission is discovering yourself, but ultimately realizing that it's not all about you. There are people in your life that you can always celebrate and serve, and that's always a reason to find happiness. Somewhere in the world, someone needs to be saved. And somewhere in the world, someone is counting on you.

7 | FOUND

"Most people waste the best years of their life waiting for an adventure to come to them instead of going out and finding one. They succumb to the status quo and dream of life being different someday. Plagued with indecision, they wait, unsure of the right path to follow. And as they wait, they miss an opportunity to live"
-Viktor Frankl

Shad was ready. He sat in a seat where many had sat before – those who did their best to downplay rumors or clarify jumbled up information, and now it was his turn. Three morning show hosts peppered him with a litany of questions, and he wasn't afraid to answer any of them. He even opened up about wanting to end his life. Shad Moss (known in the entertainment industry as Bow Wow) seemed at the time like he was at his wit's end. He didn't feel like he had much purpose anymore and shared his thoughts with DJ Envy, Angela Lee, and Charlemagne tha god on the nationally syndicated morning radio show *The Breakfast Club*:

What people don't understand is like, I done lapped the world eight times, and it's like—me being, coming into the game young, and seeing so much and doing so much, and—sometimes I just question life, like 'Damn, what else is there for me to do?'...I've done everything that I've really wanted to do... now it's just like, 'What's the next phase?'

I felt it for Shad when I heard those words. Many people have a checklist of things they want to do in their life – people they want to meet and places they want to go. Often, it's just the thought of these things on their list that satisfies them, and they remain content with their complacency. After doing everything that he set out to do, Bow Wow seemed *lost*. But how could he find himself again?

SERVING THE WORLD

U.S. psychologist Abraham Maslow's hierarchy of needs lists levels of human essentials for survival and satisfaction. If you look at those needs in a pyramid format, the lowest level is physiological – the need for food, water, warmth, and rest. Babies unashamedly remind us of these needs, along with residents of assisted living facilities. The next rung up in the hierarchy are safety and security needs, some of which have already been discussed throughout this book. Above that is the need for belonging and love. We want intimate friendships and tribes of like-minded people to connect with. Once you establish that sense of connection, you float higher up, grasping at the need for prestige and accomplishment. And when you feel accomplished, you reach for the pointiest part of the pyramid, self-actualization. Here is where you achieve your greatest potential and feel a sense of completion. Here is where we welcome *"Ever Since that Day"*, the final part of the storytelling spine.

FINISH THE STORY

At one point, I was heavily into writing poetry. Back in college, I was often asked to write pieces that dealt with whatever world issue was going on at the time. Sometimes, I was lucky enough to share whatever was on my heart. I remember having one of these heart-share moments during an evening event. Usually, my work was complete long before I had to present, but this time around I couldn't finish the job. I had the audience heavily invested in my rhetoric and then my poetry book had run out of ink.

"Sorry guys, I didn't get to finish it."

You could hear the sighs in the crowd and my heart followed suit. I hate disappointing people. There was no worse feeling than being called to the stage with your art, only to not have all the work leave your heart. Sadly enough, I didn't finish the poem and the story was never wrapped. *I'll get back to it soon,* I told myself, but the days became weeks. And then months. And then years.

How many of us are afraid to finish our story? Afraid to reach *And Ever Since that Day*? Anything having an ending may bring us fear because it forces us to turn to something new. But what if ending our story is just an invitation to begin a new one? What if the current season of your story is waiting for you to get to the finale?

DON'T ROMANTICIZE YOUR VICTORY

Have you ever seen those older gentlemen who still rock the bellbottom-shaped sideburns even though they were in vogue over 40 years ago? It's like they went to get their hair styled one time back in 1974 and said to themselves, *"This is it. I'm never changing this style again!"* Sometimes, it's dangerous falling in love with an event that changed a major part of our lives. Yes,

131

some of these moments are major turning points for us, our families, and communities, but there's a dark side to every victory. We romanticize moments and become stuck in time. This prevents us from seeing anything novel as a good thing, and over time we grow risk averse. Change often stokes the fear that we've left the best part of ourselves in the past. But what if the best part of yourself is just beginning? What if you're finally unfolding – becoming the person you were always meant to be? We have to be careful not to be so in love with where we came from that we forget to shed light on where we're going. This is how companies like RadioShack, Blockbuster and other businesses fizzle out. Once we become a Goliath in our industry, it's hard not to fall in love with what got us there.

When you share your story with people, it's important to have a destination, but most people are invested in your journey. It's what keeps people in movie theaters for over two hours and sparks Monday morning conversations. They are afraid of boredom, the lull, the negative space in between their commentary. Suffice it to say, they desire drama. Drama is the fuel that moves human emotion. Drama thrives in dialogue. It is parasitic – always searching for a nerve to disrupt. And if you haven't found yourself when drama comes, it will feast in perpetuity on your insecurities and assumptions.

There is a price for finding ourselves, sitting on the throne, and becoming Goliath in our field of interest. We obsess over the first steps on the other side of the finish line. We romanticize what got us the victory. We build golden images of thick sideburns, mullets, and flat tops. We stuff shrines with framed college degrees, family recipes, and weekly video rentals. Nothing's supposed to change once we find ourselves, but by thinking that way, we amputate innovation. What was once a new experience fades into nostalgia and new Davids come along – hungry, precocious, and gathering stones for their sling.

A DAY OF MEANING

I want you to take every gram of your imagination and visualize this. Distract yourself from your distractions and ask yourself, "What would a day of meaning look like?" For me, it would be any day where I am able to flip someone's frown. Any day where I can be fully invested in the unselfish needs of another. Those that lose sight of this lose themselves. They float around from shiny object to shiny object, trying to keep themselves distracted enough to not check in on their insecurities. And many of those insecurities are connected to the belief that they don't have what it takes to serve others. That's all purpose really is - service. Using what you have to meet the basic needs of others. In my opinion, that's what Shad was struggling to rediscover in his interview on The Breakfast Club. Up to that point, he had checked off everything on his list that served him and seemed to have lost sight of the fulfillment of serving others.

Let's get back to visualizing your day of meaning. You're the hero, and people need "saving." Someone needs their faith restored. Another's dealing with low self-esteem. Another anxiously sits on the ledge of a 5-story building, wondering if their existence has any merit left. Somehow, they're waiting for your service – some herculean act that's rooted in your love and care for others. And when your day of meaning ends, you find a way to replenish and wake up the next day to do it all over again.

Many have no choice but to string together these days of meaning. We call them soldiers, marines, doctors, nurses, firefighters, teachers, policemen. But these professions aren't the only ones that serve. We are all called to string together days of meaning. When you're reviewing PNL spreadsheets in your cubicle, how are you best serving others? When you're flipping burgers in the back and smelling like vegetable oil, how are you best serving others? When you're selling lotions, potions, and oceans, how are you best serving others? First, we have to listen to our hearts. Then we have to listen to others *with* our hearts.

How do you listen with your heart? By living in your heart. How do you live in your heart? By not making every decision based on logic. Logic will keep you in your head. It tells you that your villain is too strong, your problem too tough, your mountain insurmountable. Logic makes us live in our head. And when we live in our head, we mess with other people's hearts. But when we live in our heart, we'll mess with other people's heads. Their logic won't comprehend our bravery, our trust, our love.

MINE YOUR BUSINESS

The Gold Rush began in 1848, when flakes of gold were discovered at the base of the Sierra Mountains near Coloma, California. A man named James Wilson Marshall was building a water-powered sawmill for the founder of a colony now known as Sacramento. Word of the gold flakes would soon spread, bringing thousands of men from across the other states to join in the quest for riches. Many of these men would leave their families and jobs just for a chance to discover gold. These men were called '49ers (hey there, San Francisco!).

I have never been to a goldmine, but I can imagine its allure to those who are hoping for a life-changing discovery. What if I told you that you don't have to go very far to find a goldmine? Look in the mirror and focus on the space in between your ears. I believe that there's at least one million dollars of an idea deeply embedded in your gray matter. It's up to you to figure out how to extract it. The real question is, do *you* believe it too? So many of us will spend years of our lives with all this gold in our heads – ideas that could benefit and bless communities, countries, and continents – yet we're too afraid to mine it. We'd rather mine other people's spaces and audit their successes and failures before we mine our own business.

James Marshall was at the right place, right time, and on the early end of a wealth trend. He was the first in the region to discover a resource that would be worth fortunes for many Californian settlers in the mid-1800s. If you believe it, then no matter when, you're always in the era of a gold rush. It's time to start panning for those gold flakes in your mind. Someone's waiting for them to be found, for *you* to be found.

You are sitting on a gold mine. There are so many products, TV shows, books, recipes, and other solutions that the world can't receive because it's collecting dust – in your mine. You have so much more value than you think, and you need to share it with the world. Stop spending so much time in other people's mines. It's dark, confusing, and has treasure that doesn't belong to you. Now go and mine your own business!

YOU'RE FOUND, NOW WHAT?

I have two sets of Apple AirPods. Now you might think this is a bit over the top but let me explain. I remember coming home from work one day, only to realize that my AirPods were not in my pocket. "*I must've left them at work,*" I thought, but when I went to work the next day, I couldn't find them. I looked in every possible place around my workspace, but nothing. I asked colleagues and building security but was just met with shrugs. My AirPods were lost. I felt sad because my wife bought me those AirPods for my birthday, and now I had to own up to their loss. I finally gave up and went to a local BestBuy to purchase another pair of the expensive earphones. Months would pass as I would enjoy my newly minted pair until one day – I would lose the second pair as well! There wouldn't be another purchase this time after looking "everywhere."

One day I was cleaning out my car – vacuuming the seats and floors, wiping down the dashboard, etc. I was getting ready to put the vacuum away when something impressed me to look under the driver's seat. I had checked under my seat a few times already as I had vacuumed it clean, but this time around, my eye caught something deep in the crevice of a small opening in the driver's side floor. Something small. Something white. Sure enough, it was my AirPods! And based on the unique markings and scratches, I could tell it was my original pair! I never let them out of my sight again.

The end of the year came and after months of having our home on the market, we finally got it sold. (For those of you who've moved before, you know how hectic it can be – buying and labeling boxes with clothes, kitchenware, and the like all over the place.) We began packing away the clothes in our closet. As our closet became more and more bare, my eye caught something nestled right into the bottom of one of the closet corners. Something small. Something white. It was my *second* pair of AirPods! Both of my discoveries (or should I say, "recoveries") taught me two things:

1. **We're never really lost, we're just misplaced.** I know I started out this book by having you realize that you might be lost, but the reality is that you're just misplaced. Like the AirPods, you were created with a purpose to serve but something happened and set up a rift between who you currently are and who you're meant to become. Sometimes the discovery of yourself comes after a long period of a frantic search. Other times, you find yourself after one swift inkling.

2. **We find ourselves when we *move* ourselves.** The only way I was ever going to find my second pair of AirPods

was when I was prepared to transition from one place to another. I couldn't just *think* myself into another season of my life. I had to take action, and taking action required me to clear out familiar spaces. Spaces that stored items of comfort. Items and keepsakes that were piling up and serving the shelf more than they were serving me. It wasn't until I was able to fully clean out what was comfortable to me that I found the misplaced item that was created to serve me.

There will be times when you're so lost that the only person on earth who can find you *is* you. You'll continue to search for yourself in the places you spend the most time, but it won't be enough. Sometimes, it won't happen on your watch, but in a divinely orchestrated moment that was meant for you and God. And if you listen closely enough, you'll realize that you were never lost, just misplaced. Under a car floor. In a closet corner. Or whatever place you need to rediscover yourself the most.

Speaking of Apple products, I'm sure everyone who has a Mac has at some point come face-to-face with one of the most menacing villains ever – the Spinning Rainbow Wheel. I've had to fight it a few times just writing this book! The Spinning Rainbow Wheel usually shows up when there are too many applications open. Your MacBook will start to vent, cooldown, make noise, and do everything in its power to return you to the program you were working on. With all that the computer's trying to process, it feels frustrated, overworked, and overwhelmed. In other words, it feels *lost*.

Can you feel the Spinning Rainbow Wheel in your brain sometimes? The tension of work, family, friends, and your own needs all demanding parts of your daycheck? You don't want to let anyone down, so you open up the work app while the marriage app runs in the background. The kids' app is hard to close, so you leave that open too. It's a trip to the Mental Mall all over again with a twist. Suddenly, you realize you have too many apps open. You start to vent as you try to cool down your internal processor that's now running at an unsustainable pace.

When too many areas in your life demand lots of your energy at the same time, you usually don't have enough in you to meet all their needs at once. So, what do you do? With a MacBook, there are typically two options it needs to do to find itself again – either shut down the computer completely or "force quit" the app. In this case, I don't want you to shut down, but I do want you to think about force quitting.

No one likes a quitter, but in this case a force quit is usually the best way to get your computer running again. When there are too many things running on my MacBook and the wheel pops up, I right click (or two-finger click for some) on the program icon and the option comes up to force quit the application. The *force quit* shows no mercy to anything else going on in the background. It is the one command outside of shutting down the computer that immediately exits you out of that program. After force quitting the applications taking up a lot of your computer's power, it tends to return to normal. No more wondering how you're going to function in one or two applications. And most importantly, no more Spinning Rainbow Wheel.

As we've discussed before, your story will be filled with many occasions where it feels like everyone and everything is taking your air without much consideration and you can't breathe. Your force quit will put an immediate end to the demands of what needs you. This is often for your sanity. If you're a mother with a full-time job and the moment you get home there are kids that need your attention, a force quit looks like a weekend getaway while your spouse, parents, or trusted guardian picks up the slack. If you're a C-suite executive that needs to micromanage every detail of your department, a force quit looks like delegation to the next colleague in command. Or if you're an employee that's working for a C-suite executive and feeling undervalued with no room for growth in the company, a force quit might just look like... quitting. There are times when quitting is the only option. It's the decision that brings you back into balance with your being, your presence, and your purpose.

THE ARRIVAL OF OUR RIVAL

Ursula. Jafar. Cruella. Scar. The voice. The lamp. The pups. The champ. All of these Disney villains desired something that the protagonist had, and because of that, they set out to take out their competition. All of our rivals are usually looking for something that will change their current situation at the expense of another's livelihood. For your rival, *you* happen to be their greatest impediment. Halt a drug dealer's supply? You're their rival. Become more popular than the head cheerleader? Rival. Stop a despot from taking over a country, better yet the world? You guessed it. Rival.

Rivals are your personal villains. They draw their lines across from you early and often, opposing most of your perspectives and pleasures. They take joy in seeing you stuck. They won't admit it openly, but they often covet your character, wishing they had the ability to overcome their obstacles without rage or revenge. Our rivals are fueled by their emotions, chasing status, power, or whatever nourishes the most fragile part of themselves – their ego.

We are now at the climax of your journey, the *Until Finally* part of your story. Your villain has either just revealed themselves or finally confronted you face to face without any guise or gambit. They have run out of both monologues and minions. It's time to strike.

But here's the rub – you need no weapons to strike your villain down. There's no silver bullet, no secret concoction, no magic ring to vanquish in the flames of Mordor. For years, we looked at our villains as someone who's hurt us, abandoned us, or blocked our progress at every step. We think they sit in on parent-teacher conferences, hold offices of government, and hide behind keyboards. I'm not saying that none of this could be true, but what if your real rival was actually... you?

Think about it. A lot of Disney's villains aren't killed by the hero. They're taken down by their own greed, power or character. Simba didn't kill Scar. Scar's foolishness did. Pongo and Perdita didn't take out Cruella. Her raging covetousness did. The Beast didn't off Gaston. Gaston's bloodlust did. Sometimes your greatest villain looks nothing like the person or system you've been pinning it on, and is shaped, speaks, and saunters around just like you.

What you have not realized until now is that you've had the power to tell your villain all this time to go away. To rest and not be woken. But your power was buried deep within your inability to actualize your true potential. You're more powerful than the words or wounds anyone has spoken or inflicted against you. Now's the time to defeat your villain. Tell yourself:

I am stronger than my deepest insecurities.

I am more beautiful/handsome than anyone can imagine.

I am validating myself, and therefore need no validation from anyone else.

I am accepting myself for who I am and who I am becoming.

I will shed light on the darkest parts of myself in order to heal myself. No longer will these dark parts dictate my character.

I am free. No chains – whether physical, mental, financial, or spiritual will convince me otherwise.

I was created to serve and love without fear.

I will forgive myself, forgive others, and ask for forgiveness wherever needed.

I am declaring victory over my past, and in every current and future moment of my life, simply because I choose to.

And may this choice help serve the world for the greatest good.

This is your declaration. Say it repeatedly – in your head, on paper, and out loud until your villain is defeated.

Our villain's fall is determined by our ability to fully acknowledge and remember who we are. When we forget who we are, we give our villain the victory. It's when we are confident enough to stand in our purpose, our service, and our cause that WE, not our villains, are victorious. And this comes with us being less polite and more honest.

THE PROBLEM WITH POLITENESS

I was coming home from school on the bus one day and was probably no older than five. I was sitting at the front of the bus next to my sister and doing my best to read the ads when an older lady entered the bus. I don't remember how old she appeared to be, but apparently it was old enough for my mother to tap me incessantly on my shoulder.

"Elroy, stand up and give the lady your seat."

"But why, Mommy? I'm tired."

"Be a gentleman. It's the polite thing to do."

"But being a gentleman is hard, Mommy!"

I gave up my seat, but apparently not fast enough to keep her belt off my behind when I got home. Being a gentleman was hard for a tired 5-year-old on a bus, and it sure seemed like it cost a lot to be polite – on both my mind and my behind!

As I got older, being polite became easier. I would smile at folks, say hello, and really mean it. *"You catch flies with honey,"* were the thoughts my mother drilled into my head as I made sure to respect my elders and feelings of others. But I realized that politeness would only carry me so far as I started yet again to analyze my own relationship with others.

Had I been too polite with myself and everyone around me? And not honest enough?

Let me explain. It would seem like a normal desire for us to want to hang around polite people. Polite people will welcome you into their space. But *honest* people? Honest people will tell you from the jump that they want no new friends and will spare you the energy of being polite. As time goes on, politeness drains the energy needed for deeper and more intimate relationships.

Politeness says hello and smiles deeply. Politeness wants no problems and will do its best to convince others that there are none. The problem with this is that the algorithm of human behavior tells us that at some point, our smiles will dwindle. With nearly 8 billion people on the planet, someone will do something that's out of alignment with our values and preferences, and if all we do is smile, we don't effectively communicate how we feel. This sends the wrong message to our community members because remaining polite at all times never exposes them to your raw emotions – the honest you.

Soon, we realize that we no longer want to hang around just polite people, and we want to hang around *honest* people. Honest people will tell you about the spinach hanging in your teeth, about smelly breath or underarms, or ask why you keep choosing to remain in your mess. They won't allow you to maintain the comfort you've chosen if they see it as detrimental to your development. Unfortunately, we spend a good amount of time around polite people because it allows us to stay at the level we feel most safe or comfortable. It's light, fluffy, playful, and doesn't require much introspection or deep dives with others.

After several rounds of politeness, the people you're hanging around may want a bit more. They'll ask themselves, "When is it time to stop being polite and start being honest?" And if you call these people your friends, it looks like you have to begin asking the same question – not just with them, but with yourself.

When do I stop being so polite to myself and start being honest?

When we're nothing but polite to ourselves, all we do is make concessions for our behavior. Politeness is the first, second, or third hit of the snooze button on a Monday morning. Politeness scurries away from the scale or convinces us to shrug at whatever number we see on it. Politeness openly agrees with what others are saying, even when we think otherwise. Politeness concentrates on maintaining a peaceful pulse in between individuals without questioning why. Politeness is concentrated. And anything that's concentrated must be used in small doses or could be considered harmful to your health. In other words, politeness can be *toxic*.

There's nothing wrong with being polite initially, but at some point, you need to be honest. And your honesty with others can end up leading both of you into the desert. The closest relationships you have should at some point take a trip to the desert. That's where the truth-telling happens – where the heart rate begins to go up. And then when all politeness is gone and replaced with pure, healthy honesty, the heart breaks in the desert. You and the other person *must* agree to put the broken pieces together. And if the hearts are made whole again, it's filled with pieces from both you and the other individual. Intimacy has been found and the relationship has been restored. We must know the times to be polite. And we must also know the times to be honest.

It is your honesty with yourself that has carried you to the end of your story. You finally had the guts, gusto, and gumption to look in the mirror. You have taken on the hardest obstacle in your story. The bruises sting, but growth has taken place. You have made so much progress and now stand at the edge of the Story Spine. Your villain has fallen, and it is now time to head home.

THE END OF THE BEGINNING

On May 31st, 2019, a 21-year-old woman named Alexis Alford set foot in North Korea. By itself, it sounds like no major feat, but for "Lexie" this was ground-breaking. North Korea marked the 196th sovereign nation she's traveled to, claiming the title as "youngest to travel to every country in the world." Guinness has since verified her achievement by collecting nearly 10,000 pieces of evidence – from travel tickets, to witnesses, to passport stamps.

It seemed like Lexie was destined to try to break the record. Her parents owned a travel agency in California. She had saved up money from odd jobs she'd been working since she was 12. She seemed to be steeped in purpose before she could understand what purpose even meant. She was fortunate to be fostered in an environment where her parents introduced her to travel at an early age. In an article by Forbes, Lexie states that she had traveled to 72 countries by the time she turned 18 and had begun thinking about breaking the world record:

> I graduated from high school two years early and had gotten an Associate's degree from a local college. I was ready to start my gap year when I dropped the idea of going back to school and began to pursue the record full-time.

What made Lexie pursue this feat? The same thing that fuels heroes, visionaries, and hopeful readers like you. A desire for something greater that is fueled by both passion and purpose. Not everyone is blessed to figure those mysteries out early on in their story. Sometimes it takes a great loss – a bludgeoning of the heart and spirit until one can't take it anymore. They're ready to move into the next chapter of their story, no matter the cost. While Lexie had a great global adventure and achieved something extremely rare, her story doesn't end there. *Ever Since That Day* must begin for both Lexie and us. We must all journey on, ready to take on the next voyage and mission.

Time waits for no one, and therefore all chapters must end. People won't always remain in your life. Semesters will come to a close. Your current house won't always be your home. The story in the chapter must end for the greater narrative in your life to continue.

I like to say that a story is nothing more than the A-Z of Point A to Point B. You owe it to yourself to live this moment of your story in full. This chapter of your life, no matter how dark or light, needs to be penned. There will be new sidekicks for support and new villains to vanquish. You might think that when events in your life look like they're closing that it's the beginning of the end. But what if that's just a perspective? What if it's really just the end of the beginning? No matter how old or young you are, there's so much more world for you to explore. You will never fully know everything, because there's always something new to learn.

I hope you've learned something new from our journey together. I hope you've realized how much power and leverage you really have. Now take that newly discovered power and pour it into the next chapter of your story.

Once upon a time, there was an empowered, glorious person named you.

And every day...

AFTERWORD

On Sunday afternoon, January 26th, 2020, I found myself looking for Zion Williamson rookie cards on eBay to flip. He had played his first game just a few days before, stunning the crowd with 17 straight points in the 4th quarter in a span of three minutes. The life of an NBA superstar had just begun. Little did I know that in just a few more moments of scrolling, I'd get a notification on my phone telling me the life of another NBA superstar had just ended.

"WHAAATTTT!?!?!?!?!?!NOOOOWAAAAYYYY!!!"

I stared at the notification on my phone, jaw dropped, completely incredulous:

KOBE BRYANT DEAD AT 41.

A helicopter had crashed earlier that morning in Calabasas, CA and Kobe had been in it. Little by little, the reports started to make their way across the major news networks and from there, the social media feeds. Fans were crying. Reporters teared up. One sports analyst dropped an expletive in frustration during a live broadcast, telling viewers that whatever issues they had with someone, to "just let that s**t go." The hashtag #RIPMAMBA started to show up on my Instagram and Twitter feeds.

Fuel would be added to the fire as it would later be reported that Kobe's 13-year-old daughter Gianna had also lost her life, along with seven other passengers. They were pilots. Coaches. Teammates. Parents of teammates. All on their way to an AAU game.

Later that day (and in the days that followed), tens of thousands of fans would gather in front of the Staples Center to mourn the loss of the retired NBA legend. Men would become emotionally vulnerable and cry on television, sharing the stories of Kobe and his relentless work ethic. Sports journalist Elle Duncan would share the story of how he was excited for her during her pregnancy when she told him she was having a girl. He shared with her how amazing it was to have daughters and that he was proud to be a "girl dad." Another hashtag, #GirlDad would soon trend on Twitter, with daughters and fathers alike sharing stories of how special it was to be have a father-daughter connection different from any other relationship. A basketball court in the Philippines was repainted in Kobe and Gianna (Gigi's) honor. Every NBA team's next game would begin with both teams taking either a 24-second shot clock violation or 8-sec half court violation, nods to Kobe's jersey numbers 8 and 24. Soccer superstar Neymar put up the numbers 2 and 4 with their hands after scoring his next goal. NFL players prayed before the start of the Pro Bowl that day to pay tribute. A moment of silence would be had during that game where chants of "Kobe!" would eventually ring around the stadium. The 2020 Grammy Awards (which took place that evening) paid tribute to Kobe at the start of the show.

If a giant falls in the west and no one is around to hear it, does it make a sound? The answer is yes. Sometimes that sound is heard all around the world and interpreted through the lens of all those who witnessed its life. Everyone felt the sound in one way or another:

- Basketball Players: He was one of the greatest to ever play the game.

- Fans: NOOO! Not Kobe!

- Reporters: Kobe was a legend. I remember when Kobe...

- Mothers: Those poor babies! I can only imagine what Vanessa (his wife) is going through!

- Fathers: I couldn't imagine that being my daughter!

- Teens: Gianna was only 13! That could've been me!

- Gigi's Teammates: That could've been us!

I could go on and on. From the African American, Chinese, Italian, and Latino communities. From aspiring basketball players and athletes alike. Kobe Bean Bryant's work ethic was unmatched, so much that it became its own legend, the "Mamba Mentality." Outside of a mourning wife and three other daughters, this is the legacy that he leaves behind.

I challenge you yet again to look at your story. You may not know it, but there are many others that look to you for what to do (or not do) when it comes to moving forward in their story. People are counting on you, so think about who you might be letting down by not doing what you've been called to do. And when your story ends, what will they say about you? What will your supporting cast, adversaries, and everyone in between have to say?

I'll leave you with this. Campsite rules often say to leave nothing behind when it's time to go. But no matter how many "campsites" you stop by in this life, you will always leave something behind. It's up to you to decide what that "something" will be.

May you be blessed as you venture further out into the landscape of your story.

Made in the USA
Monee, IL
11 November 2020

47220867R00085